CHAN
& DE

Peter Dickinson

CHANCE, LUCK & DESTINY

An Atlantic Monthly Press Book

Little, Brown and Company

BOSTON   TORONTO

FIRST AMERICAN EDITION

Library of Congress Cataloging in Publication Data

Dickinson, Peter
    Chance, luck, and destiny.

    "An Atlantic Monthly Press book."
    SUMMARY: A collection of anecdotes, stories, facts, and activities relating to chance, luck, magic, witchcraft, and fortune-telling.
    1. Occult sciences—Juvenile literature. 2. Chance—Juvenile literature. [1. Occult sciences. 2. Chance] I. Title.
    BF1411.D53   1975   133   75-28403
    ISBN 0-316-18428-4

ATLANTIC-LITTLE, BROWN BOOKS
ARE PUBLISHED BY
LITTLE, BROWN AND COMPANY
IN ASSOCIATION WITH
THE ATLANTIC MONTHLY PRESS

PRINTED IN THE UNITED STATES OF AMERICA

Line drawings by
Victor Ambrus
and
David Smee

CONTENTS

Magic and Witchcraft

Destiny

CONTENTS

CHANCE, LUCK
& DESTINY

START HERE This book is about Chance and Luck and Destiny, with Magic to bind them into a ring. Readers like me will probably have begun in a dozen other spots before they read these words, leafing to and fro haphazard. That's all right. The book is meant to be read that way too. But . . .

For those who like to begin at the beginning. Chance and Luck and Destiny—aren't they all the same thing?

A shepherd walks slowly up a yellowish-green glen that reaches into a parched mountain flank. A sudden inexplicable panic scattered his flock as he drove them out to pasture at dawn—it was just as though they smelt a wolf. He rounded up most of them without trouble, and his dog is now guarding these while he looks for the last five. They might be anywhere on the mountain, but the first places to search are those where they'll find grass to eat, such as this glen.

The afternoon air is breathless, though the quiet seems to crackle with heat. A real sound catches his ears. He stops and listens. It is a faint, shrill bleat—but he has lost no lambs and the noise is not quite that quavering cry, though it is something almost as familiar. He hesitates, then starts up the hot, shaley slope.

In the shadow of a slant rock the baby lies, wrapped in a tight-swathed roll of fine linen with a thread of gold woven into the hem. It is not yelling for hunger, but because it is pinned to the ground by a bronze spike driven through both heels. It looks about a month old.

With hands deft from a thousand lambings the shepherd eases the spike from the flesh. But then he hesitates and stands up, leaving the baby still squalling. It is a common practice in his country for parents to leave an unwanted child to die in this way— though parents who can afford cloth such as the baby is wrapped in can hardly be too poor to feed an extra mouth. It goes against the grain of shepherding to leave new-born life to die, but what parents do to their children is their own affair, especially if the parents may be rich and powerful.

As he stands there a movement on the opposite slope of the glen catches his eye—a sheep—another—all five. They are grazing in a cleft where some spring keeps succulent a few tufts of grass, a place so narrow that there is only one spot on the entire mountainside from which the shepherd could see into it, and that is where he is now standing.

The omen decides him. He lifts the baby and carries it with him while he rounds up his strays, then takes it back to his hut where he puts sheep-salve on its wounded heels and allows it to suck from the udder of his favourite ewe.

This is part of an old story. Later in this book the history of that baby is told in full, and elsewhere details are used to illustrate this and that. Here it shows some of the differences between Chance and Luck and Destiny.

Chance The flock scattered at random, and so obeyed the laws of chance, which meant that most of them were easy to find but a few more difficult. The shepherd understood the nature of sheep, so he didn't search the mountain at random but took what seemed the best chance of finding them. However, it was an unlikely chance that the baby's cry led him to the one place from which he could see them.

Luck In his month of life the baby had known both good luck and bad, until—as luck tends to—luck had evened out for him. Most children in that country were born in hovels, but he'd had the good fortune to be born in a palace. Then he'd been unluckier even than those other babies when his parents' rejoicing had turned to horror and he'd been taken away to die. But now luck had settled to its average, and he'd come to a hovel after all.

Magic The shepherd didn't believe in random happenings, because to him everything that happened was the work of some God. So that evening he made a magical sacrifice of wine and oil to thank the god who had led him to the place from which the sheep could be seen, and another sacrifice of bread and bitter herbs to ward off the anger of any god he might have offended by taking the baby.

Destiny The baby, asleep on the lamb-fleece beside the sour little fire, carried an enormous destiny, the death of a king, the rescue of a city from a monstrous enemy, plague in that city, and yet more death. All these things had already been chosen for the baby, and what had happened on the hillside that day was all part of the intricate machinery that would cause that destiny to be fulfilled.

CHANCE

rain on a sheet of still water
grains of spilt sugar underfoot
hiccoughs
small children in a playground
cloud-shadow
passing cars

The man crossed the mountain near the peak, so that he could see the sea far off to left and right of him. Now he was out of his own territory. But mountain tops are holy places, not to be soiled by the thing he had to do. He shifted the sleeping baby on his arm and started down the slope.

A long spur of the mountain lay in front of him. Too open, he thought. It'll be seen. I must find a quiet place lower down, under some rock. Which flank of the spur? No odds. I'll watch that puff of thistledown and go whichever way it goes.

From the flanks of the spur the heated air sidled upwards, meeting along the top in a series of eddies. The thistledown wavered and spun. The man watched it, glad to put off for a few more moments the action he was committed to. At last

a chance flaw in the wind took it to the left, down the slope, only a few inches above the ground, as fast as a walking man. He followed it, still watching, till another chance flaw shot it skywards and it lost itself in blueness.

As he walked on looking for a suitable rock, the bronze spike in his wallet thudded and flapped against his hip.

CHANCE   CHANCE   CHANCE   CHANCE

Your chance in life; a chance meeting; sheer mischance; chancy; no chance of the sky falling; the chances of drawing an Ace and a Jack.

Behind all these meanings lies the idea of something uncaused, or unplanned, or uncontrolled by reason, a random event.

So let's start with random events, and strange unplanned coincidences, and odds, and especially our own relationship with chance, our fear and distrust of the random mess of happenings and our desire to find patterns and causes and laws.

Chance does obey laws. In the true sand-deserts the sand is so fine and dry that you can pour it out like water, and even wash in it as though it were water. The dunes move in vast, slow waves, driven by the desert wind which lifts each individual grain and drops it somewhere else, at random. There is no possible way of telling when any particular grain will be picked up or where it will be carried to, but for tens of miles the dunes follow one exact shape—a smooth rise, a ridge as sharp as the corner of a box, and a steep, wrinkled fall—as though they had been stamped out by one giant die. Then an outcrop of rock, or an upwelling of moisture, or the hidden ruins of a sand-swamped city will interfere with the operation of pure chance and the pattern will be lost.

As you read this, every molecule of air between you and the page is jostling about at random, at quite high speeds. There are millions of them there, but there seems to be no reason in logic why their random motion should not once in a while result in their all moving in one direction for an instant. If this were to happen, and the movement were towards your face, you would feel a punch on the nose as if from a glass fist. But it doesn't happen because the laws of chance forbid it.

Outside the window where I sit is a wide street. When it rains I can see the raindrops each making a small waterspout as it rebounds on the wet-silk tarmac. In a light shower there is space enough between each drop for a man to stand, though the spaces move as fresh drops fall; but it looks as if, supposing I chose exactly the right path, I ought to be able to walk across the street, moving between the raindrops without one of them touching me. Again the laws of chance forbid it.

There are two great laws of chance, and each has a mirror image which is a law of life. The first law says that random events are bound to even out in the end, and its mirror image says that if events don't even out they aren't random.

These laws are easiest to illustrate by games of chance, but there's more to Chance than playing games. That's why the story that follows (illustrating the first law) is about a game of dice; but the one after that (illustrating the mirror image) is about a young man playing with death.

THE ABBOT'S DICE

In a crowded large room in Paris, in 1643, the Abbé de la
Bosque sits alone at a table in one corner. The lamps and
candles smoulder; cobwebs dangle from the gilded
furnishings; the people, though they are all noblemen, stink.
Mostly they are playing noisy games of cards, but the Abbé
sits in silence, tossing his beloved dice from hand to hand,
and occasionally throwing them on the table. A pale young
man, a newcomer, strolls over to watch. The Abbé pays no
attention to him—just as the hunter in the jungle learns not
to look directly at his prey until he is near enough to strike.
At last the young man speaks.

"May I sit in this chair, Monsieur?"

"Certainly, certainly," says the Abbé, as if he were thinking
about something else. He throws dice for a while more, left
hand against right, as though that were the most important
thing in the world. The young man makes polite conversation.
The Abbé barely answers. But suddenly he seems to notice
the young man.

"You would like a game of dice, Monsieur?" he asks, as
though the notion had only just dawned on him.

"If you are willing," says the young man.

"Very well, very well," says the Abbé politely. "Let us
play as follows: we throw in turn, but no matter who throws,
if the dice show a number nine or above I will pay you two
Louis; if they show a number eight or below you will pay
me one Louis. It is an even chance, you see—you have eight
numbers to lose on and I have four, so I pay twice what you
pay. Or perhaps you would prefer it the other way round?"

The young man frowns over the problem, until suddenly
it strikes him that he has only seven numbers to lose on, as it is
impossible to throw a One with two dice.

"I am content," he says.

Invisibly the Abbé relaxes. There is no need for him now

to conjure his loaded dice into the place of the pair he has
been playing with. This young man, he thinks, is no mathematician—he doesn't even realise that one has more chance of
throwing the middle numbers than the end ones, because
there are more combinations of dice that add up to the middle
numbers—there are only two ways of throwing Eleven and
only one of throwing Twelve, but there are six ways of
throwing Seven and five each of throwing Six or Eight.
In fact the Abbé ought to be paying the young man about two
and a half Louis for every time his numbers come up. Now,
if they play long enough, by the Laws of Chance the Abbé
will win. The Abbé is very interested in the Laws of Chance,
which is one of the reasons why he prefers to play with un-
loaded dice. (The other is that if he gets caught playing with
loaded dice, the stinking noblemen will have him cudgelled
by their servants, breaking half the bones in his old body.)

So they settle to play, and continue until a drizzling dawn
breaks over Paris. At the end of that time the young man
has been unbelievably lucky—he is only twenty Louis down,
when he ought to have lost three hundred. Still, he is sulky
about his losses, being no mathematician.

The Abbé smiles and bids him a polite good-bye, then
totters home to his lodgings where he enters the results of
the night's play in a ledger he is keeping. One day he is hoping
to retire from the gaming-tables and write a great treatise
on the laws of chance. He isn't bothered at all by the young
man's run of luck; if he plays long enough he is bound to hit
a streak like that, but it will all even out in the end.

DICE

The best story about their invention comes from the ancient Greeks.

"The people are starving," said Atys, King of Lydia.

"True," said his wise men. "The harvests have been so poor that there is only enough food to feed half the people. It follows that half the people must die."

"No, it does not," said King Atys. "I hereby order and decree that I and all my subjects will eat only on alternate days."

"The people will be very restive on days when there is no food," said the wise men.

"And so shall I," said the King, "unless you immediately invent something to take our minds off our stomachs."

The wise men frowned. There are few things more disturbing to wise men than a restive king. Suddenly an old throat coughed.

"I have been making some mathematical observations with a pair of cubes, marked on each surface," said the cougher. "Their behaviour does have a certain fascination. Suppose I were to wager your majesty that in three throws with a pair of these cubes he cannot throw them so that the same markings appear on both upper surfaces . . ."

For eighteen years the King and his subjects ate on one day and gambled on the next. Then the King sent for his son, a thinnish young man.

"I have been thinking," said the King. "It appears to me that our series of poor harvests can no longer be put down to a whim of chance The climate has permanently altered, and Lydia will never support more than half the people it did when I was a lad. So I suggest we divide the population between us, and one of us takes his share to seek another country."

"My father is the fountain of good sense," said the Prince.

"But do you propose that I should forsake my inheritance? That would hardly be fair, as you have already enjoyed a long reign."

"Well, let us dice for it," said Atys. And they did, and the Prince lost, and sailed away with half his people, and conquered a stretch of good land in Italy, and became the first king of a people who were later called the Etruscans.

The Greeks tended to credit the semi-mythical Lydians with all good inventions, from musical instruments to ball games. But the earliest known European dice are found in Etruscan tombs.

Princesses of ancient Egypt, two thousand years B.C., were buried with sets of dice to amuse them on their journey through the land of the dead. These dice still fall perfectly true. But all over the ancient world common people gambled mainly with the knucklebones of cloven-footed animals. These are called astragals, and are roughly brick-shaped, with rounded ends, so that there are only four possible throws. Because its flat sides are irregular, an astragal tends to land most often with the side called Vizier uppermost, so that only scores one point; the two sides that touch the Vizier are called Baker and Thief and score four and three, and the least common side, opposite the Vizier, is called King and scores six.

A few shops sell real astragals. I have also seen plastic ones. The knucklebone out of a sheep's foot will do, but the one in a lamb's foot is often still too soft. Most sheep carcasses reach the butcher's with their feet already removed, so anyone wanting to make his own astragals would do best to go either to a slaughterhouse or to a farmer who kills his own sheep. Then it's just a matter of slow, smelly boiling.

The mirror Image of the first Law of Chance says that if apparently random events don't even out, then some cause is affecting them and they are not truly random.

COUNT SERGEI'S PISTOL

Autumn, and a mourning wind weeping across the vast, sad plains of Russia. Count Sergei Balashov is not merely sad, he is bored. Surely no young man in history has been so drenched with boredom, abandoned out here to look after the family estate while his father revels at the Czar's court in St Petersburg? Miles south across the plain, in the evenings, Sergei can see a faint moving feather of smoke where a steam engine leaves the little town of Propolsk and rattles along the brand new railway towards Moscow.

One evening, watching that signal, Sergei determines to bring a flush of excitement into his own life. He takes down from a shelf his father's pistol-case and lifts out of it a revolver, a very expensive toy, beautifully made and balanced. Sergei loads one chamber with a live round, checks that the others are empty, spins the cylinder, puts the muzzle to his temple and pulls the trigger. Click! He is still alive. The feather of smoke fades westward along the darkening horizon.

All next day Sergei feels the stimulus of the coming moment of danger, and after the click of the hammer falling again on to an empty chamber he is happy and relaxed and glad to be alive. And the same next evening, and the next. He knows he has one chance in six of blowing his brains out, so when on the sixth evening he feels the cold circle of metal against the stretched skin of his temple he needs all his will-power to pull the trigger.

Click! He is still alive, and the train still moving away.

Now he is frightened in a different way. At supper he drinks no wine and afterwards he tries to work out the odds against his living through six rounds of his deadly game, but

even sober he is no mathematician. So next morning he rides
to Propolsk, where he hauls the schoolmaster out of his class.

The schoolmaster is a thin, tired, ragged old man, who has
spent his life in devising plots to assassinate the Czar, but has
never found time to leave Propolsk and put them into action.
Count Sergei pretends that he wants the information for a sad,
sad story he is writing, but the schoolmaster sees through the
pretence and rejoices. Here is a chance to strike a blow against
the hated aristocracy without even leaving Propolsk, without
even telling a lie.

"Noble sir," he says, almost grovelling, "on the first night
your hero would have five chances in six of not killing himself,
and the same on each individual night that follows. To find the
total chance on six successive nights, you must multiply five
by itself six times, and divide that sum six times by the
number six. Let me see . . ."

Here he scratches with his cane in the mud by the school-
room door.

" . . . yes, in six tries your hero would have almost exactly
one chance in three of not killing himself. In twelve nights
he would have once chance in nine. In eighteen one chance in
twenty-seven, and so on."

"I understand," says Count Sergei, frowning, and without
a word of thanks he rides home across the soaked and
squelching plain. He frowns all the way. One chance in six
of blowing his brains out is an amusing risk, but two chances
in three is stupidity. He resolves to play with the gun no more.

But winter comes. Snow lies deep across the plains. In the
forest the wolves wail. Life is more boring than ever—even
the Moscow papers do not arrive. Sergei is unable to keep
away from the gun. It is like a drug. Sometimes he does not
touch it for two whole weeks, and then, night after night, he
faces death, alone in the dusty dining-room. He keeps a diary
of this long duel, and on the sixth of January he leaves back

through it and finds that he has now failed to blow his brains out forty-two times. Slowly he calculates the sum, and discovers that the odds against his having survived so long are something like two thousand to one.

It is a moment of revelation. Even though he is no mathematician, Sergei realises that these odds are too steep to be true. Something has kept him alive. He believes that he has been deliberately spared to achieve some great work in the world. He decides to start by ridding the forest of wolves.

So he rides out next morning into the forest, gay and careless—so careless that the wolves get him. They are very hungry at that time of year.

Moral

Sergei was right in thinking that the odds were too steep to be true. So he did the normal human thing, which we all do when we see a pattern develop in the great mess of chance—he looked for whatever it was that was causing the pattern to develop. Unfortunately he didn't look far enough, or rather near enough. If you put a single round into a chamber of a really well-balanced revolver and then spin the cylinder, the weight of the round will spoil the balance and tend to carry that chamber to the bottom; so the chamber at the top, which is the one on to which the hammer falls, will almost always be empty. If Sergei had held his pistol upside down he would have blown his brains out six times in six.

This two-step process—first the pattern, then the explanation —is how we try to reduce the power of chance over our lives. All intelligence, at however low a level, tends to take the first step. An octopus has a fairly primitive brain system, but one can give it a nervous breakdown by messing about with a pattern it thinks it has discovered. Suppose for several weeks I lower into its tank either a white triangle or a black circle;

whenever the octopus touches the triangle I give it food, and whenever it touches the circle I give it an electric shock. Slowly it discovers the pattern, though it is incapable of conceiving the cause (in this case, me). It learns to touch the white triangle when it's hungry and not to touch the black circle at all. Then I reverse the pattern, and it has to re-learn the procedure. Then I break the pattern up completely, doling out shocks and food at random and occasionally showing it circles and triangles of the wrong colour. For a short time it will experiment to find a pattern that works; when the attempts fail it will have a nervous breakdown. Not only will it leave the circle and triangle alone, but its own behaviour will start to become unpatterned in other ways. It will cower, change colour, make sudden attacks on empty areas of its tank, squirt out its ink-cloud at nothing, tie its own arms in knots. Quite likely it will then die.

It's usually said that Science consists of this two-step process, plus a third step which consists of adding fresh bits to the pattern and seeing whether the explanation still works. But in fact quite a lot of science never gets further than the first step. I have in front of me a scientific journal containing a matched pair of graph curves; one plots the number of sunspots each year over the last forty years, and the other the number of thunderstorms in that period. The curves match very well. Nobody knows why sunspots increase and decrease in an eleven-year cycle; nobody has any idea how sunspots can cause thunderstorms; but the matched graphs are quite scientifically convincing enough to act on. Next time we are due for a high count of sunspots (around 1981) we can be fairly sure the electricity engineers will draft in extra men and order extra equipment to cope with the higher number of breakdowns due to be caused by lightning strikes on the transmission lines.

LIGHTNING

The bolt from heaven falls at random. It splits the oak, or fires the church, or strikes the cattle dead, and all to no purpose, all by chance.

A big flash moves at half the speed of light, and is five times hotter than the surface of the sun.

It *can* strike twice in one place. The Empire State Building is struck half-a-dozen times in any big storm over New York. In open country there are areas which get hit far more often than others. These are called lightning nests.

Ranger Sullivan of Virginia is said to have been struck four times since 1942, losing various bits of his body from his toe-nails to his eyebrows.

A lightning flash consists of several strokes, all in the same path. The main stroke, the one we see, goes upwards.

Benjamin Franklin was lucky not to get killed, fooling around with that kite of his with its thread of wire in the cord. A Russian who copied his experiments was struck dead.

When lightning reaches the ground the current spreads in a wavering, ray-like pattern across the surface, and can electrocute anything standing near. One bolt in Utah killed 504 sheep in this way. Cattle are more likely to be killed like this than humans, as they are better grounded.

One serious text-book says that as electrocution takes place by the current racing up one leg and down the other, anyone caught in a thunderstorm should stand with his feet close together. (Or one would think, stand on one leg. And hop?)

The commonest causes of people being struck are sheltering under tall trees and finishing a round of golf.

If it's a still-air storm, move gently about so as not to generate a column of moist, warm air above your body.

Better still, lie down in a dry ditch. You are safer, though, indoors than out, even if it's only a beach hut. A car is a specially safe place.

If you are swimming, get out of the water.

Only the Arctic and Antarctic circles are free from thunderstorms. In Britain, a moderately thundery country, every square mile is struck six times a year, on average.

Florida has forty times more thunderstorms than California.

Lightning has often started a fire in a building with its flash and at the same time triggered a fire-alarm with its current.

There are several stories of a flash stripping people naked but otherwise not harming them. (Just possible, if the clothes are at the right moisture to conduct the current to earth, and to explode off the body by the sudden, brief heating.)

There are tales of fields of potatoes being cooked underground. (Also, if the ground were dry enough, just possible. Just.)

B

THE LAWS OF CHANCE

but

When events are truly random
    (Things like dice, that have no cause)
Man's best hope to understand 'em
    Seems to lie in these two Laws:

Law One Now and then a lucky throw,
             Now and then a face of woe—
             Luck may wander all about,
             Chance at last must even out.

Law Two Nothing in a chance that's been
             Can change the chances yet unseen.
             Though you've tossed ten heads before
             It's evens you will toss one more.

but

Law Two Most things have a cause behind 'em
             Though it may be hard to find 'em.
             Causes that have worked before,
             Odds are they will work once more.

Law One When Chance fails to even out
             Something's messing it about.
             Forget the odds, forget the Laws,
             Seek instead a hidden cause.

    Stands each Law upon its head:
Man's best hope to understand 'em
    (Life is more than dice) instead
Since events are seldom random

THE LAWS OF LIFE

AFTER AND BECAUSE

The rooks that nested in the trees by the castle gate cawed all through the night. Next day Mad Earl John fell into the moat and drowned. An old washerwoman remembered that the rooks had cawed all the night before his father, Bad Earl James, broke his neck on a cattle-raid. The rooks knew, said the washerwoman, and all the castle agreed.

Mrs Trotway's Ford had a puncture when she was hurrying to the station to meet Mr Trotway. Getting home she found that her beagle had eaten Mr Trotway's supper. She was furious about both these things, but she laughed aloud with relief when she heard a tinkle of broken glass from the bathroom, where young Dickie Trotway was playing a game he'd invented with a soapcake. Mrs Trotway is certain that accidents come in threes.

My daughter, Phil, is a good driver—better than I am, in my opinion. But because she's under twenty-five I have to pay extra insurance if she's to drive my car; the insurance company's computer shows that in the past drivers under twenty-five have had more accidents per head than the rest of us. I sometimes think that if that computer were to spit out a figure which showed that tall blonde girls whose names began with P had an even worse record than other under-twenty-fives, the company would charge Phil even more. They'd claim to have found some sort of reason for the bad record (as they have with the under twenty-five thing—lack of experience, high spirits, and so on) but that reason wouldn't be the reason for the extra charge. Really they'd be arguing that something that has tended to happen in the past will tend to happen in the future.

I said earlier that there are two great laws of chance, and each has a mirror image which is a law of life. The second pair of laws say this: unconnected random events that have happened are no guide to unconnected random events that will happen; but few events are really unconnected and random, so even when we can't discern the connections and causes it makes sense to assume that what has happened will go on happening.

(Even where events are random, one has to think clearly about connections. If you roll a dice four times and get a six each of the first three times, that doesn't in any way affect your chance of getting a six on the fourth throw. But if you deal yourself four cards and the first three are aces, you now have less chance of getting an ace for your last card than you had of getting an ace for your first, because then there were four aces in the pack and now there's only one.)

My three examples, the castle washerwoman and Mrs Trotway and Phil's insurance, were meant to demonstrate the range of this mirror image, from pure superstition through a vague feeling that many of us have to a system that everyone would regard as quite reasonable. The following story, which is near enough true, is a more elaborate example.

THE RED HILLS

Opsim is a black boy, one of a wandering tribe who live on the edge of the desert in North West Africa. (The time is about 1930.) The tallest men in the tribe are less than five feet high. Both men and women have faces striped with a pattern of scars, made by the priest at the several ceremonies that marked their growing up into full membership of the tribe. They wear no clothes, but the women have heavy iron anklets and bracelets, according to the importance of their husbands. Opsim's mother wears so many of these that when the tribe moves camp she has to be helped for part of the march, but she doesn't complain because she is proud that her husband is the most important man in the tribe; he is the priest who persuades the ant-fathers to turn earth into iron. One day Opsim will be priest, so he is learning the necessary ritual to please the ant-fathers.

If Opsim fails to learn the art, or fails to please the ant-fathers, the tribe will die. For not only will there be no iron for spear-tips, and no trade with the millet-gathering people to the north; but also if the marriageable women are not weighted down with iron, then Toko-toko will steal them away.

Nobody has ever seen Toko-toko, but twice a year he passes through the area where the tribe lives. His journey is marked

by a fierce wind, blowing at one season from the north and at
the other from the south. Then red dust covers the land, and
the women hide under deer-skins, and men whose daughters
are ready to marry buy iron anklets from Opsim's mother's
brother. But Opsim and his father are out among the red
hills, performing the ritual that pleases the ant-fathers.

For many days they have been preparing for this, sleeping
on a platform in a sacred tree, so that their bodies should not
touch earth. They have worn leather moccasins for the same
reason, and eaten no food touched by women. They have
spoken to no man, and to each other only in the secret
language of the priests. Now, learning from the stars that
Toko-toko will soon be coming, they journey first to the place
of dead trees and gather bundles of straight sticks, which they
drag across the desert to the home of the ant-children.

This is a strange place, a flat small plain between two arms of
the red hills; the whole area is covered with termites' nests—
hard, domed, pillars, taller than a man and about five feet
thick. Opsim's father draws from his pouch three magic bones
which he throws in the air, and according to how they lie he
chooses one of the ants' nests, confirming his choice by
burning certain herbs and watching the movement of the
smoke. Then Opsim and his father laboriously hollow out
the nest, singing as they do so to tell the termites that they
are not truly harming them, but changing them from ant-
children to ant-fathers, who will go and live in the stars.
Exposed to the arid air the termites die, and Opsim gathers
their bodies into clay pots which he has brought. Then he
helps his father to pile the wood into the nest, with more
magical herbs. They fire it and seal the opening with clay.
While it is burning they go and gather lumps of red rock
from the hills.

Now Toko-toko begins his journey. He roars. In the home
of the ant-children his wind is especially strong, funnelled
between the hills. After three days Opsim's father opens the

top of the ants' nest and puts in the red rocks they have brought, together with fine white earth and more herbs, and finally the bodies of the ant-children. Then he cuts another hole in the side of the nest, so that Toko-toko may pass in through there and out through the top, and blow the spirits of the ant-children up to join their fathers in the sky.

Toko-toko roars through the charcoal. He is angry at being interrupted in his journey, and his anger turns the burnt black sticks red, and makes the red rocks glow like the sun. Opsim and his father feed the anger of Toko-toko with more burnt sticks, and more red rocks and herbs. They are not afraid of his anger, because they despise him as a wife-stealer, and they know the ant-fathers hate him and so will protect them.

When Toko-toko is gone, Opsim and his father go back to the sacred tree again, and sleep in the air, and purify themselves for eight days. On the ninth day the whole tribe travels to the home of the ant-children and watch Opsim's father open the nest. Before their eyes he lifts out lumps of strange rock, streaked with yellow and purple and pitted like a honeycomb. Suddenly he cries aloud. The tribe shout, and he shows them a dark, reddish object, heavier than stone. It is iron. And another. And another. Each time the tribe shouts.

By the time he has finished the tribe is richer by nearly twenty pounds of pig-iron, which is given to Opsim's mother's brother to forge into rings and spear-heads and anklets. It is the reward which the ant-fathers have given to the tribe for their piety and labour in sending the ant children to the skies.

One year, about 1930, a European party comes to the area and makes films of Opsim's father at his work. They find that his method of producing iron involves seventeen separate processes, all of which he believes to be equally important. Of these only five are scientifically essential: the coarse

charcoal provides the heat and carbon monoxide, the ants'
nest makes an efficient blast-furnace, and Toko-toko provides
the blast; the red rocks are high-grade iron ore, and the white
earth is powdered limestone which joins with the impurities
in the ore and floats up when the iron melts and sinks to the
bottom. If Opsim's father could make coke, he would be
able to extract more iron from the ore, but as it is his methods
are much more effective than those of most primitive iron-
smelters. The only thing is that he doesn't know *which* of his
methods are effective, so he daren't leave any of them out.

The exploration party does a survey of the home of the
ant-children, counting the nests which have been excavated
and turned into blast-furnaces in the past. The oldest ones
have crumbled away completely, but even so they find
traces of over four hundred, so they know that the process
has being going on for over two hundred years, and probably
much longer.

Opsim's father is too old to take in new ideas, but some smug
European explains to Opsim how and why a blast-furnace
works, and shows him how to build one without using an ants'
nest, and even helps him to construct a pair of bellows so
that there is no need to depend on Toko-toko. Soon Opsim
is making good iron all the year round, and teaching young
men of his own age the art. The value of iron falls as it
becomes plentiful, and the tribe is unable to buy enough
millet for the season when the animals go away; so they make
war on their neighbours and take the millet. Tall soldiers
with guns come from the coast to stop the war. Among the
reports sent back to the government in Europe is one on the
value of the iron deposits in the red hills.

If you go there now you will find an ugly mining settlement.
Opsim's tribe has vanished, though two of his sons work in
the mine. And the home of the ant-children has been levelled
and its termites wiped out with DDT, because they are a
nuisance.

B*

RISK AND DANGER

Although the basic laws of chance are simple—we know them as soon as we think about them—they have aspects which are difficult to accept. One is the idea of chance itself; it goes against the grain to know that we are in any way subjects of that blind and motiveless monarch. A second is that an event which happens after another event doesn't necessarily happen because of it. Third is the fact that odds apply to ourselves.

All the freezer manuals and cook-books warn one not to refreeze food which has been thawed, especially ice-cream. In how many well-run households does just that happen, and no one's dead yet?

There's a classic argument going on about the compulsory wearing of seat-belts in cars. Sometimes, the anti-seat-belt people say, they make an accident worse than it need have been, and that's quite true. But the accident figures show that these times are far fewer than the times when the seat-belt has prevented a death, or turned what might have been a major injury into a minor one.

Part of the trouble is that the odds are simply figures on paper. If one could arrange an experiment where the anti-seat-belt people could see a whole series of real accidents, and also see the proportion of belt-wearers and non-belt-wearers who walked away uninjured; and if one could then put the spectators into cars and force them to drive at speed into some obstacle; then I think most of them would fasten their belts.

The real trouble lies in the fact that very few people believe in their hearts that an accident will happen to them. Each of them is an individual, and an individual can always beat the odds. The worst driver I ever knew was an elderly cousin who never gave any signals, never got out of top gear, often failed to observe traffic lights and always drove in the middle

of the road, swinging especially wide on corners. The only time she ever had an accident her car was stationary, waiting at a junction in a perfectly legal position. It was rammed by a police car.

And I knew a fine, intelligent old gentleman who lived at the bottom of a steep lane. He never learned to re-start his car if he had to stop while going up hill, so he would put his hand on the horn and shoot out full speed on to the main road at the top of the hill. His son once took a stop-watch up there and counted the traffic and timed the spaces between passing cars. He calculated that his father had one chance in eighty of hitting something, or being hit, so he was due to have an accident in the next two years. The father had already been doing this for twenty years, and did it for another ten, before he died peacefully in his sleep.

But in the kingdom of chance single cases prove nothing. Somewhere else an old gentleman drove on to a main road and hit a bus. Somewhere else a lady remarkably like my cousin was doing sixty on the wrong side of the road when she hit a police car. Somewhere else a family is eating re-frozen ice-cream for the very first time, and tomorrow they'll all be sick.

1   How many people must you have in one room for there to be a fifty-fifty chance that two of them will share a birthday?

2   If a million hands of bridge are dealt somewhere in the world every day, how often should one be dealt in which each of the four players holds a complete suit?

3   Without taking fertility drugs, what chance has a woman of having twins at her next pregnancy?

4   How often should a comet collide with the earth?

5   In a certain country there are a thousand elephants and a million mice, spread at random over a flat, treeless plain. Seen from above, the area of an elephant is a thousand times that of a mouse. A she-eagle, flying over the plain, lays an egg. Why has the egg slightly more chance of hitting an elephant than a mouse?

5   Because some of the mice are standing under some of the elephants

4   Once in 1.3 million years

3   1 in 84

2   Once in 6,000,000,000,000,000,000 years. (In fact it happens much more often than that, because of imperfect shuffling of the pack, hoaxes, and perhaps, even, unconscious tele-kinesis.)

1   Twenty-three

Answers

ODDS

There are two languages for describing odds, the mathematician's and the gambler's. You are playing a dice-game and you need a four to win: the mathematician will say you have one chance in six, or a 1/6 chance (or he may put it in decimals or percentages); the gambler will offer you odds of five to one against. They mean the same thing.

Some gambling odds (dice, many card games, roulette) can be exactly calculated like that, some can't. Take horse-racing: in countries where bookmakers operate, they work like this. A horse called Splurge is due to run in the 3.30 at Epsom next month. It's not a major race, so little money has been bet so far. You go to a bookie and ask for the odds on Splurge. The bookie knows a bit about the horse, and guesses that he has a moderate chance, so he offers you ten to one. Later on some other punters bet heavily on two other horses; in order not to lose too much money the bookie reduces the odds on those two, making them joint favourites, and Splurge's odds go up a bit. Then a horse that has beaten both the joint favourites is badly beaten in another race, and their odds rise. Splurge comes back to ten to one, and you bet £2 on him. He actually races at eight to one, and wins, but as you bet at ten to one you get your £2 back, plus £20. If he'd lost the bookie would have kept the £2.

Most of the odds in life are much more like horse-racing than dice-rolling—a guess based on a bit of knowledge, and a hunch, and what other people think, and so on. When a politician, after landing his country in some embarrassing mess, excuses himself by saying "We took a calculated risk," he's trying to claim that he worked out the real odds against failure, and decided the stake was worth it. What he *means*, of course, is that he made a bad guess.

THE MATHEMATICS OF CHANCE

Anyone seriously interested would do better to get a text-book. Here are a few very elementary rules of thumb.

1 The gambler's language is no use for mathematics. Convert three-to-one either to a fraction or a percentage. Make it 1/4 or 25%.

2 0 or 0% then means no chance at all; 1 or 100% means certainty. Your chance of throwing a five in one throw of a dice-cube is 1/6 or $16\frac{2}{3}$%.

3 For a chance *of* a chance you multiply. Henrietta, who lives in a town containing 10,000 bachelors evenly spread through all trades, wishes to marry a red-headed bishop with one leg. Among the ten thousand there are 40 bishops, 2,000 red-heads and (owing to an extraordinary series

of accidents where a footpath crosses the railway) 1,250 one-legged men. That means 1/250th of the bachelors are bishops, and one-fifth of those bishops are red-heads, and one-eighth of those red-headed bishops lack a leg. I should have said "lacks" because the fractions, multiplied together, come to 1/10,000. Hurry, Henrietta.

4 For a chance *or* a chance you add. If Henrietta had wanted either a bishop or a red-head or a peg-leg, she could have added the fractions (which in this case simply means adding the number of suitable bachelors and dividing by 10,000). 3,290/10,000 is just under 1/3, or one chance in three, near as dammit.

5 Often the sum will only work if you calculate the chance of *not* doing something. In Henrietta's country the girl has to wait for the man to ask her, in any case; so while she's waiting she wonders what the odds are that one of the first eight men to ask her will have to go down on a wooden knee to do so. Even Henrietta can see that it's not a certainty, which it would be if she added 1/8 to itself eight times. Nor can she multiply because that would make the chance ridiculously tiny. But if she wonders what her chance is of not being asked by a peg-leg eight times in a row (which is what would have to happen if no peg-leg asked her in the first eight) she can then multiply 7/8 by itself eight times, which works out at a bit over 1/3. So her chance of being asked by one is a bit under 2/3.

The trouble is that in almost everything we do (except playing games of chance) you cannot calculate like this. You would find, if you went to Henrietta's town, that the bishops are railway fanatics, and that most of the accidents on the footpath happen when bishops are driving the trains, so almost all bishops have two legs. On the other hand you'd find that there is one red-headed bishop with a wooden leg, and that Henrietta spotted him before she announced her requirements. In which case the match is pretty well a certainty, and it's the bishop who hasn't got a chance.

The Law of Large Numbers

That's about the limit of my mathematics.

Unfortunately there is an important part of the mathematics of chance that lies beyond my limit. It describes the point at which chance, so to speak, becomes certain. In outline I understand how and why it works, but I couldn't myself do the sums. Anyway, in outline it runs like this.

In day-to-day life, chance remains chancy enough. There's a fifty-fifty chance whether the next car past my window will be coming from the right . . . No, it wasn't, but that doesn't mean that the next one *must* be coming from the right, to square things up. It's still a fifty-fifty chance.

I've just taken a coin from my pocket and tossed it ten times, getting heads seven times and tails three. That's not at all surprising—even ten heads or ten tails ought to occur

about once in every five hundred sets of ten throws. But if I carried on and tossed the coin ten thousand times, there's no conceivable chance that I'd get seven thousand heads and three thousand tails.

Of course, all I'd really get is a difference of something under twenty between heads and tails. The same applies if I went on to ten billion tries, and by then the difference would be so small a proportion of the whole that I could ignore it and say that the coin had come down exactly half heads and half tails.

This means that the larger the number of total throws, or events or whatever, the smaller is the percentage deviation from mathematical probability needed before you can say it means something, that the events are not quite random, that a hidden cause must be affecting them. The mathematics outside my limit are those used to calculate exactly where you can say, in any series of events, that something more than chance is operating.

For instance, most of the experiments in telepathy and telekinesis rely on these laws. One can't expect a telepath to guess a hidden card every time, so the experimenters have tended to set up a vast number of guesses and hoped to show that the guesser has scored significantly more than he should. The crucial word is 'significantly'. Say you set up the following experiment: you arrange for one of ten lights to be switched

If a single pair of houseflies mated at the beginning of one year, and all their eggs hatched and those flies mated and laid eggs which hatched, and so on, by the end of the year the whole earth would be covered 47 feet deep in houseflies. This is a measure of the odds against any one housefly completing its life-cycle.

on at random; the randomising is done by a radio-active source, which spits out its particles in a totally causeless and uncontrollable fashion; you then get people to concentrate on the lights, and try to influence the randomiser to switch on a particular one; after 50,000 switchings, if only chance were operating, the 'right' light should have come on 5,000 times, but in fact you find it has only come on 4,790 times, or 210 less than it should. This looks like peanuts, but apparently the odds against a deviation of 210 in 5,000 are something like 1,250 to 1; that means that you've got odds better than 999 in a thousand that chance is being affected in some way, and that your radio-active source is being 'disobedient'. (This experiment has been done, on a smaller scale, and has come up with results of about that order.)

Tossing a coin ten billion times is obviously a fanciful occupation; even guessing fifty thousand cards doesn't come very high in a list of useful things to do; but the Law of Large Numbers does in fact affect people other than gamblers, insurance companies and ESP workers, because there are random events that do happen on that enormous scale— the millions of generations of animal evolution, for instance, or the unthinkable number of atoms in a block of uranium which when added to the unthinkable number in another uranium block becomes the critical mass that will trigger a hydrogen bomb.

In 1838 Edgar Allan Poe published a story called "The Narrative of Arthur Gordon Pym", which told how four men survived in an open boat after a shipwreck, until, driven by hunger, three of them killed and ate the fourth. His name was Richard Parker.

In 1884 four survivors of the sinking of the ship *Mignonette* drifted about in an open boat until, driven by hunger, three of them killed and ate the fourth. His name was Richard Parker.

Of course, coincidences do happen, however great the odds against them.

A SLIGHT COINCIDENCE

Between two large European countries lies the tiny state of Mumberg. It is only a dozen miles across, but its inhabitants are very prosperous because it has two thriving industries, spying and betting. All the great countries of the world keep a troop of spies in Mumburg, to spy on each other, so plenty of foreign currency comes in that way. And the Mumburgers are ferocious gamblers, and have set up all sorts of pools and lotteries; originally these were for their own enjoyment, but now they too attract a lot of foreigners.

When Thomas entered the main square he had a white carnation between his teeth. In his left hand he was carrying a square cardboard hat-box containing his father's second-best hat. In his right hand he was carrying a copy of *Punch* and a paper bag full of breadcrumbs.

There was a perfectly good reason for all this. It was a National Holiday in Mumburg, so Thomas's father had told him to go to the Cultural Museum and study the paintings, but first to collect his father's second-best hat from the hat-makers. Thomas's father kept buying new hats to be his best hat, and then hating them. The only one he ever wore was this second-best hat, which he'd had for twenty years and sent once every three years to the hat-makers to be re-blocked. Thomas had collected the hat but had no intention of studying pictures. He was far more interested in studying pigeons, which he believed to be more intelligent than people. The breadcrumbs were for the pigeons and the copy of *Punch* was to sit on while he fed them.

Oh, the carnation. At the entrance to the square a flower-seller was giving flowers away because she'd just heard that

she'd won a big lottery worth 293,478 grocken. She saw that Thomas hadn't got a free hand, so she put a white carnation between his teeth. It made him feel rather a fool, but he didn't mind because he was rather a fool. His father said so.

Thomas was half-way to the foot of the enormous statue of Count Ulvar XXXIX (known to history as Mad Ulvar) when he was approached by a short, bald man wearing a white raincoat and carrying a square cardboard hat-box.

"What is in your box?" said this man.

"My father's second-best hat," said Thomas, after putting the box down and taking the carnation from his mouth.

"Good," said the man, and then simply stood there as if it was now Thomas's turn to make conversation. So Thomas said "Are you interested in pigeons?"

"Personally I prefer parrots," said the man.

"That's all right," said Thomas sincerely. He thought it quite sensible to prefer parrots to pigeons, though not Thomas's own taste. What wasn't sensible was to expect him to prefer *pictures* to pigeons.

Hoping that he had done all that politeness demanded, Thomas walked quickly on to his favourite place at the foot of the statue. Here he was soon so deep in his studies that he never noticed that the bald man had followed him, had placed his own box on the ground beside Thomas's, had peered for a while at the noble face of Mad Ulvar (although it was barely visible through the pigeon-droppings), and had then picked up the wrong box and walked calmly away with it.

Nor did Thomas see a few minutes later a flustered young man rushing about the square with a cardboard hat-box in one hand, a copy of *Punch* in the other, and a white carnation between his teeth. This young man was flustered for two reasons: first, he was late because the flower-seller had already given all her white carnations away, so he'd had to run right down to the market to buy one; second, the box he was carrying contained a secret device so powerful that if it were dropped it would blow up all Mumburg.

By that time, not far away in a steel-shuttered room at the back of a lottery office, a huge black-bearded man was weighing in one vast hand the box that contained Thomas's father's second-best hat.

"It is surprisingly light," he said in a purring voice. "Are you certain you made the right contact?"

"Certain," snapped the bald man in the raincoat. "He carried the carnation and magazine and gave the correct passwords. He was most professional. He had contrived to make himself look remarkably young, and had brought crumbs to feed the pigeons. He was very cool."

"And you were not?" purred the big man.

"In this raincoat! And carrying a box which if dropped would blow up all Mumburg!"

The big man made a sweeping gesture of disdain.

"Hey, careful!" yelled the bald man.

He dived and caught the box just before it reached the floor. Then they both sat down, pale and trembling.

Meanwhile, a few streets north in a steel-shuttered room at the back of the Br*t*sh Embassy, a slim man in dark glasses was talking to the head of Department G, who was known as GG.

"They made contact," said the slim man.

"What did they say?" asked GG.

"Couldn't hear, sir. A pigeon sat on my microphone at the crucial moment."

"Bad luck. What did they do?"

"Couldn't see, sir. They went round the wrong side of Mad Ulvar's statue."

"Rotten bad luck. Never mind, you've done very well. Time to knock off now."

GG rose from his desk and reached for his hat. He clapped it on his head, snatched it off again and stared at it in disgust.

"Mad Ulvar's statue, eh?" he said suddenly. "That's in the main square, isn't it? My boy Tom's been there today, studying the pictures in the Cultural Museum."

"Great Scott, sir, what a perfect cover! Oughtn't we to make use of him?"

"No go, I'm afraid," said GG solemnly. "I don't know where he got it from, but poor old Tom's a bit of a fool."

Meanwhile the flustered young man had ground his teeth so much that he had chewed up his carnation and was wondering what to do. He could not make the long trip back to the laboratory at − − − − − − − −* because they would have realised by now that the device was missing. They would follow him to Mumberg. He must flee, but he must cover his tracks. The first thing was to leave the device where it would not be noticed for a while, but would later be picked up by a street-cleaner and tossed into a dust-cart. BOOM! If Mumburg were blown to bits just after he left, no one would be able to pick up his trail.

Casually he crossed the square and slid the box under the flower-seller's barrow. She was now giving away orchids.

By this time, in the steel-shuttered room at the back of the lottery office, the two spies had recovered their nerve sufficiently to open the box. The large man stared down into it with angry eyes.

"That is not what I call a device," he purred. "That is what I call a hat. A rotten bad hat."

He snatched it out of the tissue paper and flung it at the bald man, who caught it and began to examine it with unbelieving eyes. He read the name inside the brim.

"Thunder and lightning, sir!" he squeaked. "This hat

*Name too top-secret to print.

belongs to the head of Department G in the Br*t*sh Embassy!"

"So?" purred the big man.

"It is his famous second-best hat, sir. There has been an error, but we can turn it to our advantage. The makers have put fresh stiffening inside the lining—if we were to replace that with one of our new cephalic aerials, we would be able to read directly the thoughts of the head of Department G."

The big man tugged thoughtfully at his beard, but carefully in case it came off.

"You don't like it, sir?" said the bald man.

"I suppose it is worth a try," said the big man. "But I am worried, worried. In your absence I have learnt that there has been a serious error committed in the front office. As you know, we had arranged for the man who brought us this device to be paid 293,478 grocken in the form of the first prize in our lottery. However he did not want the publicity, so we changed the arrangements and you took the money to him this morning. But front office were not informed of the change, and have now told some woman that she has won that sum. Head Office will not be pleased to learn that we have expended twice the agreed sum, and have only one hat to show for it."

"Then you must tell this woman, sir, that there has been some mistake in her coupon."

"Excellent, excellent," purred the big man. "You have saved my life. In return I shall not strangle you with my bare hands, which is what you deserve for your mistake over the hat."

The bald man looked less grateful than he might have.

By this time Tom was so dizzy with watching pigeons that he could learn no more, so he rose to his feet, picked up the box beside him and set off across the square. His attention was still so taken up with his beloved birds that he did not notice the extra weight. However, his arm soon tired and without thinking he put the box down and stood watching the wheeling wings across the evening sky. At this moment a policeman entered the square and told the flower-seller to move on, as she was obstructing the entrance to the square by the crowd that had gathered round her for free orchids.

She wheeled her barrow a few yards. Tom politely stood clear but when the barrow came to rest it covered the box he had been carrying. So when he looked round, dizzier than ever, he saw the box which *had* been under the barrow. He picked it up, jumped on a bus and went home.

In Department G of the Br*t*sh Embassy the Duty Officer was attempting to decode a telegram. At last he got the message clear. It was from Headquarters: SECRET LABORATORY AT –––––––– REPORT DEViCE STOLEN STOP BELIEVE TAKEN BY TRAITOR TO MUMBURG STOP IF DROPPED DEVICE WILL BLOW UP WHOLE CITY EXCLAMATION MARK. The Duty Officer clicked his tongue. This was serious. It would mean ringing up GG, who hated having his evenings interrupted. Rather than do that at once, the Duty Officer settled down to decode the message again, in case it came out different.

In the square the flower-seller, having waited till the policeman was out of sight, trundled her barrow back to its proper place. As she did so she saw a nice square box lying on the ground, so she picked it up and popped it on her barrow, thinking that when she'd thrown its contents away it would be useful to keep her lottery money in.

"Got my hat, lad?" said Tom's father genially. "Excellent, excellent! Let's see what sort of a job they've made . . . great Scott, they've packed it in something heavy!"

He heaved the box onto a table, cut the string and opened the lid. He stared down at a squat orange cylinder marked with the single word 'DANGER'.

"Fool of a boy," he snapped. "What have you done with my *hat*?"

At that moment the telephone rang. Tom's father hated the telephone, especially in the evenings, so he snatched it up in exasperation.

"That you sir?" said a nervous voice. "I'm afraid we've got a telegram about a missing device which Head Office seem to think is in Mumburg, sir. I decoded the message three times, sir, and it always came out the same, so I rang head office and they say it's an orange cylinder marked 'DANGER'. Apparently if it's dropped it could blow up the whole city."

"OK," said Tom's father with brisk
assurance. "You can ring them again and
say that we have the whole matter in hand,
and they can have their precious device back
tomorrow."

"Very good, sir."

"Now, look here, this is important. Send
your very best agent out to the main square to
make enquiries about a box with a hat in it, left
there some time this afternoon. Don't make a mess
of it. The safety of the world depends on you getting
it right, see?"

"Very good, sir."

All down the telephone Tom could hear the Duty Officer's
heels click. Tom's father swung back into the room with

such impatience that he caught his foot in a rug, stumbled, clutched at the table and managed to knock the device on to the floor. It fell with a dull thud and lay still.

"Typical Br*t*sh workmanship!" snarled Tom's father. "When it's dropped it's supposed to blow the whole city to bits."

"I expect they mean when it's dropped from an *aeroplane*," said Tom.

G's best agent found nothing in the square because by that time the flower-seller had pushed her barrow home and was discussing with her mother the best way to spend the lottery winnings. But on his way back to G he met in the doorway a short, bald man wearing a raincoat, and carrying a square box.

"What have you got there?" he said.

"A hat," said the bald man. "I understand that the gentleman who wears it works in this building."

"You're very helpful," said the agent. "I'll take it up."

The agent hummed happily as he filled in his "Mission Successful" report. GG never allowed his agents to fill in any other kind of report, but it was a pleasant change to be able to do it truthfully.

Next morning GG strode into his office and found his hat in a box on the desk; eagerly he unwrapped it and tried it on. He frowned, snatched it off and looked inside the lining.

"Stupid idiots," he muttered. "They ought to have realised I always take the stiffening out. Fancy bit of work this time, too."

Carefully he worked the cephalic aerial free and dropped it into his machine for chewing up secret documents, which coughed twice but chewed it up in .093 seconds. Then he placed his precious hat on his head and settled down to a day's spying.

In the steel-shuttered room at the back of the lottery office the bald man fiddled with the knobs of a cephalic wave receiver. Not a light winked.

"It is not working, sir," he said nervously.

"Alternatively," purred the large man, "GG does not have any thoughts in his head. I have sometimes wondered."

Meanwhile, in a suburb to the north, the flower-seller was sobbing over a telegram explaining that she had not won 293,478 grocken on the lottery after all.

"Cheer up, duckie," said her mother. "There's always that nice box you brought home. Why don't you look and see what's in it?"

Gloomily the flower-seller fetched the box and opened it.

"Why, it's a lot of money!" said her mother, beady-eyed.

"Bet you it isn't as much as 293,478 grocken," sniffed the flower-seller.

"Bet you it is," said her mother.

For every Mumburger a bet is a bet, so they settled down to count it.

"Two hundred and ninety-three thousand, four hundred and seventy-eight grocken exactly!" said the flower-seller.

"Now, *that's* what I call a coincidence!" said her mother.

YOUR CHANCE IN LIFE

If you are a boy, your chance of . . .

becoming Prime Minister is	one in 5,000,000
becoming President of the USA is	one in 12,000,000
getting your name into a history of your country is	one in 2,500,000
fighting in a war is	one in 6
marrying is	6 in 7
marrying before you are 20 is	one in 14
marrying a millionairess is	one in 600,000 (UK) one in 90,000 (USA)
living to your hundredth birthday is	one in 1,400
winning a Nobel Prize is	one in 1,250,000
going to prison is (US figures not available)	one in 800
making a hit record is	one in 25,000
being involved in an air disaster is	one in 4,600 (UK) one in 660 (USA)
becoming a Grand Prix driver is	one in 1,500,000
breaking a world athletics record is	one in 2,000,000 (UK) one in 700,000 (USA)
being struck by lightning is	one in 71,500
being a homicide victim	one in 1400 (UK) one in 90 (USA)
getting away with murder is	one in 6

If you are a girl, your chance of . . .

becoming Prime Minister is	one in 200,000,000
becoming President of the USA is	one in 480,000,000
getting your name into a history of your country is	one in 20,000,000
marrying is	6 in 7
marrying before you are 20 is	one in 5
marrying a millionaire is	one in 12,000 (UK) one in 2,900 (USA)
having triplets is	one in 9,300
having ten children is	one in 3,200
living to your hundredth birthday is	one in 375
winning a Nobel Prize is	one in 35,000,000
going to prison is (US figures not available)	one in 9,200
making a hit record is	one in 300,000
being involved in an air disaster is	one in 25,000 (UK) one in 2,900 (USA)
breaking a world athletic record is	one in 1,200,000 one in 1,600,000 (USA)
being struck by lightning is	one in 274,000
being a homicide victim is	one in 1500 (UK) one in 275 (USA)
getting away with murder is	one in 6

NOTE: I've made these figures as good as I can, but don't take them for gospel. Some involve more guesswork than others.

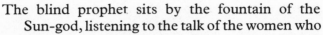

The blind prophet sits by the fountain of the Sun-god, listening to the talk of the women who come to fetch drinking-water; these days it isn't the usual babble, but hushed, fearful, often mere whispers.

"It's reached the other end of our street. One whole house gone, all in one night."

"If I was you I'd get ready to clear out. Soon as it gets within five doors, off you go."

"But where? You can't tell where it's coming next. It's got no reason to it. Look what happened to that old drunkard, Philip. Everyone in that house went down, half of them died, he never had a qualm, excepting it was hangovers. Worthless old sot. I doubt if water's passed his lips these ten years. You can't say a God's causing the plague because he's angry, or Philip would be the first he'd take, wouldn't he?"

"I don't know. I don't understand it. If only I could see some sort of pattern to it I wouldn't be so frightened. Here, I'll give you a hand up with that . . ."

The prophet listens to their receding footsteps, and the splash of the water behind him. Plague. He reaches for his staff, and at the touch of the smooth olive his inward vision begins to stir. A voice in the fountain speaks, whispering, "Here, here, here is the cause, here." The fountain of the Sun-god.

With a spasm the prophet heaves himself to his feet, crying aloud, "The God is angry. The Sun-god is angry."

His voice echoes off walls. He hears the footsteps of passers-by falter and still.

"A voice has spoken to me from the fountain," screams the prophet. "The Sun-god is angry with the city."

Footsteps surge towards him. He feels the crowd draw round him. He is raising his arms, ready to prophesy again when he hears other voices shouting, "Way there! Way there! Way for the King!"

He feels the crowd part and hears the steady pace of a large, strong man. The King's voice speaks.

"So?" he says. "Then the plague is easily cured. Let us send to the oracle of the Sun-god and ask how we have sinned. I have known the oracle to lie, but perhaps it will tell us the truth this time. Shall I do that, prophet?"

Out of nowhere a blast of terror flows through the blind man's body, like a wind off snowy peaks.

"No," he whispers. "No. Perhaps I was only dreaming. Perhaps it is all mere chance."

He sinks into the dust and listens again to the hissing fountain. It says nothing to him now.

IS THERE SOMETHING WRONG WITH THE LAWS OF CHANCE?

The Laws of Chance seem absolutely proof from attack, armoured before and behind. By that I mean that they could be attacked from two directions: by saying that there is a mistake in the reasoning that constructed the laws; or by saying that when you apply them to the actual world they don't work. But there isn't; and they do.

Though the mathematics of chance are extremely complicated, each step is simple, and the first steps—the things that we can see are true without proof—also seem quite obvious.

And wherever the Laws of Chance have been applied by science, they seem to produce results that work.

And yet still we wonder.

Mostly we wonder when we read the well-authenticated case of a gentleman on the East Coast of North America who caught a crab which had his wife's lost wedding-ring round the claw.

Or the GI from Chicago who captured a German prisoner in Normandy and found the man was wearing a watch belonging to the GI's brother, whom the German himself had captured in North Africa two years earlier.

Or the Canadian who was crouching in a dug-out when a large piece of shell-case carrying the number 26750 thumped down beside him. That was his own number.

The truth of stories like this is often hard to track down. I have several times come across the following. In the first World War, before the common use of parachutes, a pilot engaged in a dogfight had an enemy plane on his tail and started on a tight loop to escape. He was just too late and a burst of fire actually hit his plane as he went into the loop, one bullet breaking the strap that held him in his cockpit and another damaging the control wires, though he himself

was unhurt. At the top of the loop the control wires finally broke, which meant that he couldn't maintain the curve that kept him in his seat by centrifugal force; and as his strap was broken he fell out and began to plummet to the earth. However, another plane in the fight was a two-seater which had gone up without its spotter in the rear seat, and our pilot fell straight into it and lived to tell the story.

Obviously it's possible that the story is true. There's nothing in it that couldn't happen, with planes going as slowly as they did in those days. The trouble with it is that it's too good a story, too pat and too exciting. It's the sort of tale we'd all like to believe. It's also the sort of tale that's pointless *unless* it's true—anybody can invent a story of astounding coincidences, but then he'll have to tell it as if it were true, or there's no point in telling it at all.

Here's another example of the same problem, except that the details can be checked. There are plenty of versions of it. This one comes from a newspaper cutting.

In 1860 Abraham Lincoln was elected President of the USA. He died in office, shot by an assassin, who had been born in 1839. After the shooting the assassin ran from a theatre to a warehouse. He was killed before he could be tried. Lincoln's secretary, Kennedy, had advised him not to go to the place where he was shot. Lincoln's successor, born in 1808, was called Johnson.

In 1960 John. F. Kennedy was elected President of the USA. He died in office, shot by an assassin, who had been born in 1939. After the shooting the assassin ran from a warehouse to a theatre. He was killed before he could be tried. Kennedy's secretary, Lincoln, had advised him not to go to the place where he was shot. Kennedy's successor, born in 1908, was called Johnson.

That's a stunning set of coincidences, but . . . Sad to say, the newspaper stretched the facts a bit. Booth, who killed Lincoln, was born a year too early, in 1838. He was caught several days after the murder in a tobacco barn, which is only just a warehouse. He rode most of the way there. The Kennedy who tried to warn Lincoln was a policeman, and I can find no reference to Mrs Lincoln, Kennedy's secretary, telling him not to go to Dallas. However, even allowing for those details, the coincidences are quite striking. And there's another creepy detail which the newspaper didn't mention. In 1960, *before* President Kennedy was even elected, Jeremy Kingston wrote an article in *Punch* pointing out that an election year ending with the figure 0 was unlucky for American Presidents. This comes once every twenty years, and every President since 1840 who has been elected in such a year has died in office (though not always before he was re-elected for another term). Three died from natural causes and four were shot. The writer argued that a wise man in such a year runs for Vice President; he was naturally very upset when what he had written as a joky bit of juggling with figures turned into hideous truth at Dallas. Anyone who stands for President in 1980 will need to be either brave or unsuperstitious.

One striking point about this story is that the coincidences don't matter. How would history have been in any way different if one of the Kennedys had been called Kelly, and one of the Johnsons Robinson or been born in a different year?

In *The Challenge of Chance* Arthur Koestler collected a lot of weird coincidences, and they almost all had this quality of being very unimportant, not to say dull. A typical one told how a man took some friends to visit St Paul's Cathedral, and during the conversation beforehand they mentioned three different friends, one whom they thought to be living in a London suburb, one in Northern Ireland and one in Canada. In the course of that afternoon they met, separately, all three friends. There was no 'purpose' in these meetings; that's to say that nothing came of them that in any way changed anyone's lives (except that they all thenceforth became rather more respectful of the possibilities of chance).

There's no point in listing the hundreds of similar cases. As I say, they're mostly rather dull. But here's one which is interesting because it happened to have a meaningless bearing on the Allied invasion of Europe on June 6th, 1944. It's customary in modern warfare to give code-names to operations like this, and also to the places and equipment involved in them. So the whole invasion was known as 'Overlord'; the Naval part was 'Neptune'; the two beaches which the Americans attacked were 'Utah' and 'Omaha'; and the famous floating harbour was 'Mulberry'. In the month before the invasion all five of these words appeared in the same paper's daily crossword, as answers to clues. The two most important of them, 'Neptune' and 'Overlord', came on the same day, only four days before the actual invasion. The Allied Intelligence people were sufficiently alarmed to send men to question the harmless schoolmaster who compiled the crosswords.

Chance Warning

So most coincidences are trivial, and some have an almost joky quality. But there is another sort which appears to matter, but which we instantly feel doesn't really count as a coincidence.

One night in Richmond, California, the police got a telephone call. An urgent voice told them to go to the corner of St Pablo Avenue and Macdonald Avenue, where a train had been in collision with a truck. The truck-driver had been badly hurt. A squad car was sent out and found the place quiet, with no sign of an accident. They assumed that it must

Correspondent

On the Italian battlefield the crisis is far from over and it is most unlikely that Kesselring has succeeded as yet in withdrawing the bulk of his 10th Army to temporary safety past the critical point on Highway Six by Valmontone.

The struggle we are watching is no Battle of Rome. Militarily a much greater issue is at stake, nothing less than the fate of Kesselring's armies.

Gen. Alexander may decide this issue in any one of four ways, to which he may resort in combination or in turn:

By the encircling movement of his left wing, now under way, he may still trap the bulk of the 10th Army.

Secondly, he may use his armour to crash through Kesselring's rearguard beyond Frosinone, and so turn retreat into rout;

Thirdly, if Kesselring should extricate his battered remnants from the trap, Alexander may breach the "Rome Line" by a deliberately prepared attack astride Highway Six or Highway Seven (the Appian Way); or,

Fourthly, when Kesselring pulls out of the "Rome Line" with what is still left to him—as, sooner rather than later, he must—Gen. Alexander, by relentless pursuit, can turn the mountain roads to Northern Italy into a true way of tribulation.

To any or all of these developments, the fall of Rome is incidental. The overriding necessity is the destruction of the German armies in Italy.

IRISH BRIGADE LAUGHED

LEAFLET WAR FAILS

It is revealed to-day that when fighting patrols of the Irish Brigade threw out German troops infiltrating into their positions on the Cassino front at the end of April, the Germans countered by dropping propaganda leaflets in English which tried to suborn the Irishmen.

But the Irish—described as "a bulwark among veteran British Army formations"—laughed and went on fighting. The Germans then shelled the entire brigade front.

Men of the Royal West Kent Regt. were concerned in another incident of the fighting on the old Fifth Army front now disclosed. In this case bluff played a part in the destruction of a German sangar—strongpoint—by a patrol of 10 men led by 2nd Lt. Stanley Smith.

Within a yard or two of the sangar they were challenged by the sentry. Lt. Smith played for time, while he prepared a grenade, by answering in unintelligible but forceful tones.

Then he threw his grenade, which killed the sentry, and his men attacked. Another sangar and a machine-gun post were also dealt with swiftly.

Prize Competition No. 5,797

The first three prize-winners of Prize Crossword No. 5,797, published on Saturday last, were: A. Brown, Halsbury-road, Liverpool; Mrs. Hollingsworth, Finsbury Park-road, N.4; [...] rker, Woodberry-way, E.4.

The prize solution was:—ACROSS: 1. Well done; 5. Staffs; 7. Not known; 10. Common; 11. Override; 13. Childs; 14. Key; 16. Ordain; 19. Servant; 20. Advice; 21. Asp; 26. Denote; 27. Half-time; 28. Cherry; 29. Training; 30. [...] er end. DOWN: 1. Winnow; 2. Liners; 3. Dance; 4. Newark; 6. Too short; 7. Familiar; 8. Sing-song; 12. Dervish; 15. Bee; 16. One; 17. Handicap; 18. Even keel; 19. Scot free; 22. Parrot; 23. Office; 24. S[...]e; 25. Begged.

Another prize puzzle to-morrow.

large or small, to me, John A. Dewar, President, c/o Hoare & Co., Bankers, 37, Fleet-street, London, E.C.4.

PIANO wanted, grand or good upright.— Prices, &c., to L., North Ockenden, Upminster, Essex. (Upminster 433.)

SECOND-HAND FURNITURE and effects bought at HIGHEST PRICES, prompt cash. Contents of homes, hotels, offices, &c., including vacuum cleaners, refrigerators, safes.— Frederick Lawrence Ltd., 47, Westbourne-grove, W.2. 'Phone Bay. 1182.

GOVERNESSES and DOGCARTS, show condition, 40/80gns. on rail. Also Harness Heyman, 2, Cadogan-place, Sloane-st. Slo. 8161

WHERE IT IS MOST NEEDED, the Midway Mission Hospital ministers to the sick and suffering in one of the poorest districts of East London. Costs, are 25% above pre-war, have made it necessary to make an urgent appeal for funds. Will you please send a generous donation to Sir George H. Hume, J.P., M.P., L.C.C., Chairman. Austin-street, Bethnal Green, London, E.2?

WRINKLES eradicated one visit. Non-surgical. Also free for photos.—Pad. 4346.

HOWARD HOTEL, Norfolk-street, Strand.— Modern. H. & c. water in every bed room. 1st-cl. restaurant, cocktail bar. Air raid shelter.

ACTUAL USER requires Modern Car.—24a, St. Mark's-rd., W.10. LAD. 2031.

PIANO, good, wanted.—Details, price, 62, Kinveachy-gardens, S.E.7. (Woo. 0856.)

PATENTS and DESIGNS ACTS 1907 to 1942. —Notice is hereby given that on the 4th July, 1944 an Originating Summons (1944 P. No. 225) issued out of the High Court of Justice (Chancery Division) on behalf of the Pytchley Autocar Company Limited asking that the term of the said Letters Patent may be extended for a further period of one year and ten months: will come before the Honourable Mr. Justice Morton for directions as to the hearing and that any person desirous of being heard in opposition must, at least, eleven days before that date, lodge notice of opposition (giving an address for service within the United Kingdom) at Room 156 Royal Courts of Justice, Strand, London, And serve a copy thereof upon the undermentioned solicitors and upon the solicitor to the Board of Trade.
Dated 24th May 1944.
PAKEMAN, SON & READ, 43, London Wall, London, E.C.2 Solicitors
Upon whom all documents requiring service should be served.

PUBLIC NOTICE

NATIONAL HOSPITAL for DISEASES of the HEART, Incorporated, Westmoreland-street, W.1, and Maids Moreton, Buckingham. Notice is hereby given that the 87th ANNUAL GENERAL MEETING of the Governors will be held at the Hospital, in Westmoreland-street, on TUESDAY, 6th June, 1944, at 4.30 p.m. The Rt. Hon. the Earl of Cromer, G.C.B., will preside
By Order,
ROBERT G. E. WHITNEY, Secretary

No. 5,802

ACROSS

1 Era of peace, not a Chinese newspaper (two words —6, 5)
7 A saintly battle (7)
8 On a large scale (7)
10 Spanish coin (4)
11 Prove false (5)
13 Sound of misery (from a starving person?) (4)
15 With her this makes a little S. coast river (3)
17 Joint holder (6)
19 But the pretender did not make this 31 down (6)
20 Not a caddie: his job was a lighter one (7)
21 But the 27 across who wears this need not be a revolutionary (6)
23 Little feline (3)
25 Amount for a retreating scientific mouse (3)
27 This smith once stood a siege (4)
28 In one sense only we want this to describe the job of house-building (two words—3, 2)
29 This group of people may be quite respectable (4)
32 Harsh to the ear (7)
33 No visionary (7)
34 Describes Utopia, unfortunately (11)

DOWN

1 Step round the pub for a boat (7)
2 Look (as one should when crossing a road) (4)
3 Lower (6)
4 The dainty that was sampled at the bird table (6)
5 The plane for a night-flier? (4)
6 Time for a refresher in hot countries (7)
9 Sounds much alike but is just likely... (11)
12 "Cave" may be a misleading clue (7)
14 This kind of race is often a touch - and - go affair (5)
16 "Stiffen the summon up the blood." "Henry V." (5)
18 This 19 down is a cutting tool obviously (3)
19 See 18 down (but in the past) (3)
22 A nomad probably (7)
24 Poetic epithet for many an island (7)
25 English county (6)
26 Island base in the Gallipoli days (6)
30 Soft part of 6 down (4)
31 Food referred to in 19 across (4)

Y'DAY'S SOLUTION.—ACROSS: 1. Long Island; 8. Idle; 10. Democratic; 11. Ruin; 12. Edge; 15. New York; 18. Alice; 19. Erect; 20. Breve; [...] gent; 22. Poser; 23. Union; 24. Green; 25. Usher; 26. Earnest; 30. Pelt; 33. Pro[...] 34. Garden gate. DOWN: 2. Omen; 3. Glove; 4. Surly; 5. [...] ctor; 6. Dice; 7. Flag; 9. Breaking up; 10. Diving-bell; 13. Dress-shirt; 14. Enterprise; 15. Neptune; 17. Ocean; [...] Keep out: 20. Briar; 27. Aster; 28. Norse; 29. Sling; 31. Evil; 32. Twig; 33. [...] hut.

QUICK CROSSWORD

ACROSS
1 Dog
4 Disgusts
8 Serpent
9 Go back
11 Dress
12 Silly
13 As a dog does
16 Keen
18 Fruit
19 False
23 Rigorous
25 Goddess
28 Foreign measure
29 Sort of glove
31 More pleasant
33 Required
34 Sarcasm
35 Measure
36 Affectedly coy
37 Deceases

DOWN
1 Astute
2 Choice morsel
3 Weird
4 Cleaning stuff
5 Shopkeeper
6 Cower
7 Weapons
10 Make certain
14 Possessed
15 Firm refusal
17 Examination of accounts
20 Subjects
21 Untruth
22 Shaved down
23 River
24 Outer coating
26 Severe
27 Gibes
30 Angry
32 Unemployed

Y'DAY'S SOLUTION ACROSS: 1. Willow; 4. Pastor; 7. Stratagem; 9. Lute; 10. Dare; 11. Steel; 13. Drench; 14. Rounds; 15. Squint; 17. Cutter; 19. Solos; 20. Noun; 22. Adam; 23. Superfine; 24. Render; 25. Render. DOWN: 1. Walled; 2. Lute; 3. Wrath; 4. Player; 5. Seed; 6. Ravens; 7. Strenuous; 8. Magnitude; 11. Scans; 12. Lotus; 15. Sandal; 16. Topers; 17. Confer; 18. Rumour; 21. Nude; 22. Anon.

Printed and Published by THE DAILY TELEGRAPH Ltd., 135, Fleet-street, London, E.C.4; and at Withy Grove, Manchester, 4.

be just another hoax call, made by some idiot for the fun of hearing the siren and the tyre-squeal. Still, they poked around for a while and were just getting ready to leave when a train came roaring through. The tracks crossed the road but the driver of a passing truck didn't notice the warning lights and failed to stop. There was an appalling smash, and just as the voice had said the driver was very badly hurt. In fact it was lucky for him that the police were already there to rush him to hospital.

Now, that could be coincidence, because such hoaxes are not uncommon. But most people wouldn't think of it like that. Depending on their own cast of mind, they'd say either that it was a genuine mysterious warning, or that the whole story was untrue. The mysterious-warning idea doesn't have to mean that it was an unearthly voice speaking on the telephone; it could still have been a hoaxer, bored, unconsciously receptive to whatever it was that sent the warning, or else unconsciously catching a glimpse of the future event. The hoaxer would have to tell *some* story, so it would only need a little jog to make him tell the right one.

There are plenty of similar 'warning-voice' episodes. Sometimes the voice speaks. There was a miner in a deep mine in Pittsburgh, Kansas, who was crawling along a passage when he seemed to hear a voice say "Stop!" He stopped. The voice said "Quick! Go, go!" Terrified, he crawled back the other way and into a side opening. At that moment the roof came down in the passage where he'd been, falling with such force that the rushing air put out his lamp. But his friends found him safe.

Just after the first World War a woman was sitting in London. Outside was a dense November fog and it was bitterly cold. Suddenly, without knowing why, she got up and ran out into the street without even stopping to put her coat on. She ran blindly for some distance along the pavement and found a dying man. He had been gassed in the war, and the fog was too much for his ruined lungs. She could do no more than wait with him while he died.

The Kind Current

If it is hard to accept that things like the 'warning-voice' stories are chance, because they seem to matter too much, what are we to make of extraordinary flukes which don't matter at all? They seem to disobey the laws of chance, but also to be so meaningless that it seems almost easier to assume that the laws of chance are wrong.

But suppose the laws are right, but at the same time there is a drift, a bias in all nature, away from complete randomness and towards the beginnings of a pattern. If you set up a computer to trace a completely random path through a network of connections (imagine yourself going into a maze; the first passage splits into two; each of those splits; and each of those; and so on; by the time you have passed a hundred splits there will have been over a million ways you might have taken through the maze) well, you'll find your computer will tend to stick to a surprisingly small number of possible paths. Dr Stewart Kauffman of the Massachusetts Institute of Technology has constructed random 'networks' of connections which can connect themselves up in any of a very large number of different ways, but keep changing. He found they refuse to change at random, trying out all possible connections; instead they go through a small number of connections and start again. If you mess around with them, putting them in unfamiliar connections, they get back quickly to the ones they 'know'.

There is even some evidence that this drift towards patterned behaviour is a drift in favour of life. Two scientists, Walter J. Levy and Eve André, fixed an infra-red lamp over a group of baby chicks and connected it to a device that switched

C*

it on and off at random. When it was on the chicks were happy; when it was off they were miserable. Left like that over a long period, the lamp switched itself on more often than it switched itself off. But when they took the chicks away it stopped behaving like that and switched itself on and off an equal number of times.

They tried the same experiment using first fertile eggs and then hard-boiled eggs, and got a similar result. Where there was life, the lamp was 'kind' to it. Where there wasn't, it didn't care. The 'kindness' was very slight—about one per cent—but it was there over thousands of switchings, a drift, a tendency.

Suppose this drift exists all through the apparently random chaos of matter, a faint current carrying all things towards order, favouring what is already ordered, especially what is ordered enough to be a living thing—then the place where we would expect to find evidence of it is in the realm of life itself. In the countless species of living forms, from ants to elephants, from mushrooms to oaks, all of which are patterns and all of which became those patterns out of the mess of chance, surely there must be clues.

Egg-talk

"I wish the light wouldn't keep going on and off."

"*What do you mean, the light? That's not a light, it's the great, good, all-wise, all-merciful heat-god!*"

"I think it's just a light and goes on and off at random. There! Now it's dark. Brrrr!"

"*Of course it goes out if you say blasphemous things like that! Oh, great Heat-god, warm us again! There!*"

"Ah! That's better! But I still think . . ."

"*Shhh! Do you want it to leave us in the dark for ever?*"

CREATURES OF CHANCE

Every begetting is a throw of the dice. I inherit myself from a human ancestry, and that makes me man; but I inherit half myself from my mother and half from my father, and there is no calculating how those halves might have been otherwise arranged, or how many other men or women I might have been, all with the same parents and the same instant of conception. Chance chose that I should be me.

Man is a very large species, with a lot of variation between members. In other species of less size or complexity Chance may have less scope. In the 1890s there were only about twenty Northern Elephant Seals left in the world, living off the coast of California. But steps were taken to preserve them and now there are around 30,000. Even so, the species is not safe, because they all inherit themselves from a very small stock of ancestors, so there is very little variation in the genes they can pass on. That means that if their environment changes they will have less chance of adapting to it than a species with a big common pool of genes, which can produce variations which will thrive in a changed world.

This is something to be born in mind when we set ourselves to rescue any species that is in danger of extinction. The great Blue Whales that browse the plankton in the Antarctic currents, the hump-backs that sing their weird messages beneath the waves—it isn't just a matter of stopping the cruel hunting. For hundreds of generations after they are made safe from the harpoon they will need all the luck that nature can give them if they are to maintain their difficult lives in the slowly changing oceans.

Chance does not only play its part in that throw of the dice at the moment of conception. It also acts—sometimes very dramatically—in the mutation of an individual in a species. Each of us inherits from our parents a pattern or template which, so to speak, instructs the embryo how to become

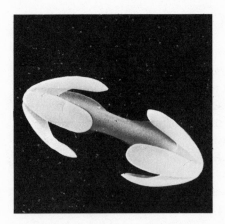

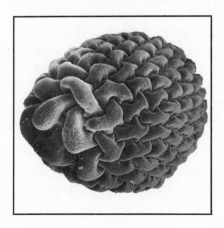
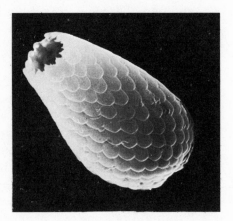

The Patterns of Life. Some of the shapes revealed by the electron microscope. Above: *Spicule of sponge* ×4410; *Moth's egg* ×1160; Below: *Mite's egg* ×950; *Shell of amoeba* ×3070

human. We pass a similar template on to our children; so for the most part a species can only inherit from the pool of genes that already exist among the older animals of that species. But from time to time something happens to change the template between one generation and the next, altering the position of one molecule and so adding a new gene to the pool. It may be a cosmic ray chancing to strike just there or a dose of X-rays; or some form of atomic radiation, man-made or natural; or even some chemical influence; but the result is a mutation.

Many mutations are harmful, so much so that the individual does not live to breed and pass the gene on. Many are minor and neutral, but they add to the gene pool and may come in useful some day. Very, very few are immediately advantageous.

And even then it is hard to say what is harmful and what is advantageous. The normal hamster is a little mouselike thing with desert-coloured fur, which helps it to hide from predators in the hawk-ruled deserts of Persia. There, gold fur would

mean almost instant death, so perhaps that mutation has occurred many times in the past. But the environment was against it. Then the environment changed, in that a species of ape evolved which took a fancy to small, cuddly, cute, gold-furred creatures and was prepared to pamper and protect them, and so the mutation became an advantage. In fact it is said that all the golden hamsters in the world are the descendants of a single mutant female.

So evolution is a process whereby sheer chance, acting innumerable times in a number of different ways, produces creatures as diverse as the reticulated giraffe, the archer fish, the white ant, the aye-aye, the marsupial mole, the liver fluke, and man. The rest of this section is mostly an account of some of these creatures, chosen for their sheer oddness of form or behaviour. Every one of them, I feel, deserves a dozen exclamation marks, but I cannot keep throwing up my hands in wonder and amazement.

Scientists and mathematicians say that since the world began there has been time enough, and chances enough, for all these life-forms to have evolved only by the laws of probability. But, harking back for the moment to what I was saying a few pages ago, if there *is* in all matter a drift towards patterns, towards life, towards greater and greater complexity of life forms, that would be an easier explanation for many of us to accept.

Flukes

(A creature with a name like that clearly has a place in a book like this.) There are lots of flukes. Their place in nature is somewhere along with worms and slugs, but they live inside other animals and most of them cause unpleasant diseases. Their life cycle goes through several stages. Many flukes have to spend some of their stages in snails and some in mammals, and their big problem is how to transfer from one to the other. The flukes that live in water-snails can swim out into the water and rely on being drunk by a passing sheep, but there is a species that lives in a mud snail that has had to incorporate an extra host into its cycle. When its time has come to leave the snail it causes the snail to cough out sweetish blobs of jelly, which contain hundreds of the fluke's next stage. The jelly is attractive to ants, which eat it and with it some of the flukes. The flukes then move through the ant's body and invade its brain-cells in a way which alters the ant's behaviour. Normally an ant has a very rigid behaviour-pattern, but an ant 'taken over' by flukes forgets all that and simply climbs a blade of grass and clings there, night and day, until a passing sheep chooses to munch it up, blade, ant and fluke, all together.

The Poison Tongue

Collectors of sea-shells prize the shell of a large snail called *Conus*. A good specimen of *Conus Gloria Maris*—the Glory of the Sea—might sell for several thousand dollars. *Conus* snails are flesh-eaters, and several live by catching fish, despite their own slow movements.

Fish sleep, but even asleep a fish is a wary creature; one

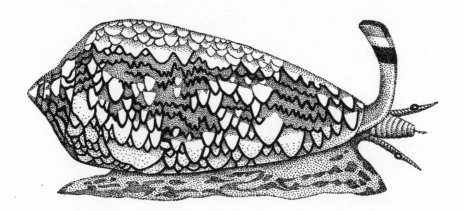

tremor in the water and it's away, darting between rocks. But the snail's slowness is an advantage, because it allows it to come close without disturbing its prey. When it's in range it floats out its long, slim tongue and very gently caresses the fish, like a poacher 'tickling' a trout, while it feels for the tender place behind the fin. Conus carries a poison dart in the tip of its tongue, and as soon as it is ready it jabs it through the skin. The poison is quick-acting. The fish jerks twice, and is dead. Conus then sends out a tube towards the body, folds the fish double and sucks it down the tube.

Strange Harem

In the Great Barrier Reef lives a type of fish whose normal domestic set-up is that one male patrols and defends a section of reef, which is his territory. He is extremely aggressive towards any other male fish who come anywhere near, and also fairly bullying to the half-dozen females who live in his territory and constitute his harem. In the harem the females are aggressive to each other, in strict order of precedence, with the head wife bullying the rest, and so on. If the male dies, sometimes the males on either side extend their territory and take over the females. But more often the head wife becomes violently aggressive to the other wives and then, within a week or so, changes sex and takes over the territory and harem herself—or rather himself.

Pop-Gun

The archer fish, Toxotes, lives in the estuaries of far-eastern rivers. Its food is the insects which it shoots down from overhanging branches by spitting a blob of water at them. To do this it has evolved a mouth like a water-pistol, with a funnel-shaped groove along the roof. Its tongue can be cupped below this to form the other half of the funnel, and the tip of the tongue curls up to close the narrow end. When it builds up pressure in the wide end of the funnel and then lowers the tip, the water squirts out a jet which is accurate at distances of several feet. Toxotes has evolved eyes which can focus through the water-surface; without these its tiny water-cannon would be useless.

Artists in Crime

The satin bower-bird of Northern Australia has a complicated
mating ritual. All the bower-birds build a special sort of
dance-floor where the male can perform for the female, but
the satin bower-bird both paints and decorates his. First he
makes an avenue of twigs and sticks, which he daubs with
black paint made from his own saliva mixed with any soot
or charcoal or other dark, powdery stuff he can find. He uses
a stick as a paint-brush. Then he ornaments the floor of the
avenue with bright objects—petals, pebbles, bits of broken
glass—with a strong preference for anything bright blue.
If, in the course of looking for these, he comes across another
satin bower-bird's bower he vandalises it, smashing the
building and stealing as many of the bright objects as he can
carry away. An ornithologist once numbered a lot of little
bits of bright blue glass and left them on his lawn. Within
a few days they were all gone. He managed to keep track of
some of the bits as they moved from bower to bower, and
found that the best ones sometimes got stolen several times
in a single week.

A Few Oddities

In New Guinea there are snails that can jump, by beating the end of their single foot on the ground.

Most squids when attacked squirt out a squid-shaped blob of ink which doesn't merely serve as a smoke-screen but also confuses the attacker by its shape and its smell. Some squids confuse him still further by changing colour as they flee. Deep-sea squids have no use for 'ink' because the water is already black and lightless, so they squirt out a luminous blob to dazzle the light-shy predator.

The Grebe, a diving bird, can submerge without a ripple by expelling all the air from its feathers. It just ceases to be buoyant and sinks like a scuttled ship.

Nobody knows what the toucan's beak is for, nor why parrots are almost the only creature beside man that is strongly left- or right-handed.

The spitting cobra, like *Toxotes*, is accurate up to about six feet. It aims its little jet of poison at the eyes of its attacker, and can blind a large animal.

Most male spiders have trouble mating before the female eats them. Some solve the problem by bringing her a dead fly. Some wrap the fly up in a parcel, so that she'll take longer to open it and eat it. Some just bring her a very complicated parcel with no fly in it at all.

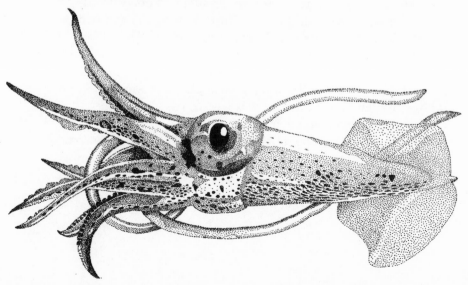

THE PATTERN MAKER

The list of curious life-forms could go on for ever. Zoologists say that wherever there is a living to be got, there will be found some creature getting it. They speak of that creature filling an 'ecological niche'. I prefer to think of life as a tide flooding up a many-creeked inlet, with a main expanse of water, broad branching channels, narrower ways, and at last the remote ditches and backwaters into which the fringes of the flood reach out. The map of this inlet is laid out not in the dimension of space but in the dimension of time.

There even appears to be a process whereby a group of species that is nearing extinction (seeping into its final channel) starts to specialise with frantic abandon, as if searching for some way further. The early dinosaurs were clean-looking, efficient beasts; it was shortly before they all died out that the more bizarre ones evolved, the ones with curious neck-frills or unnecessary horns or elaborate ranks of plated spines. At a simpler level there was a type of fossil shell which remained much the same for millions of years, a plain, flat coil; then, all of a sudden, it tried a whole series of new shapes, double coils, spirals, even straight lines. Then, just as suddenly, it died out. It had reached those last ditches at the fringe of the tide.

This image of a tide—it is only an image—brings me back to my main question. Is something continually happening which is more than mere chance? Chance *is* like water—it finds its own level. Below that level it fills every cranny, above it it leaves all possibilities untried, every inch of land dry. But a tide, though it is only water, has a moon to heave it above the level, to pull it slowly westwards.

Does life have such a moon?

Left to itself matter ought, by the logic of chance, to become more unpatterned, more chaotic. And so it often seems; clean steel becomes rust, rocks become dust, the exact fretted lacework of a snowflake lasts only a few seconds before it is vague water.

But even chaotic matter seems at times to be working to pattern itself—into crystals, into rainbows, into self-repeating chains of molecules. And once those molecules have become life there seems to be no limit to the urge towards a greater and greater complexity of pattern and behaviour.

To believe that there may be something beyond plain chance, something that draws the tide of life towards itself, isn't necessarily to believe in God, or a God-like force, that is interfering with the chaos of matter, pushing it into patterns and inventing jumping snails for light relief. By the laws of chance dice need only to be very slightly uneven and in the end the unevenness will tell. In the same way the moon that draws us can be very far off and still, at last, we will drift towards it.

LUCK

a stone in your shoe
an empty eggshell on the grass
a wink in church
a telephone that stops ringing just as you reach it
a voice laughing behind a closed door
a missing tooth

The childless queen leans over the cradle, gazing
at the   chance-found baby. Her hair is grey now, but
she remembers how glossy-black it was when
she had first come to the palace, a healthy,
handsome girl, chosen by the king
because he loved her, but welcomed by
everyone else because she looked the type
to produce a strapping male heir.

She remembers the years of disappointment,
the whispering courtiers, every one of whom seemed to have a
buxom sister or cousin, sure to produce a stream of sons. She
remembers her husband's love and patience.

And now they have been rewarded for their love. It is as
fine a boy as any king could ask for, pink in his sleep, with
tight, dark curls beginning to hide the smooth skull. The
wounded feet are healing, without any infection, their
swelling less and less as each week passes. And his arms are
strong, strong enough to hurt when he tugs at a handful of
grey hair. He seems everything a prince should be, even to the
angry and imperious frown that at this moment tightens the
small forehead.

"Oh, we have been lucky, lucky," whispers the queen.

The old slave-nurse glances at her, sideways. Doesn't she
know it's unlucky to say things like that?

CAESAR'S LUCK

Chance evens out in the end. But between whiles it runs unevenly, and to the mathematician good luck is only a name for the periods when chance is running well, and bad luck for the opposite swings.

When it's happening, though, it seems like more than that. In a period of good luck you feel stronger and cleverer than usual, and the colours of the world are brighter, and you wake eagerly to each new day, knowing that it will bring you no problem you cannot beat. Luck, to people who believe in it, is far more powerful and mysterious than chance. Card-players given the choice will always prefer to play against a skilful player than a lucky one—at least they can match skill, but there's no defence against luck.

Julius Caesar was a great soldier. He planned with care, he picked good officers, he looked after his men, he judged well the moment for caution and the moment for attack. But what his soldiers valued most was Caesar's Luck. Even the results of good generalship they put down to luck. He used his luck as a propaganda weapon. When in the end he had to fight other Romans, his enemies were more afraid of his luck than of the courage and discipline of the seasoned army that he led.

He halted his horse on the bank of a river. This side was
Gaul, where he was the legal supreme commander. The other
side was Italy, where he was nothing but a private citizen,
and guilty of high treason if he led armed men one yard upon
that land. He smiled his dry little smile, nudged his heels
against the horse's flanks and rode into the water. The ford
was shallow at that season, and the river foamed no higher
than his horse's knees. Legion by legion, singing the obscene
marching songs that soldiers always sing, his army followed
him across the Rubicon.

Caesar turned to his chief of staff, cocked his head and said,
"The dice are thrown now."

As the sentence, repeated down the line, ran through the
army it was followed by cheering and guffaws. Old Caesar,
old baldie, was gambling on his luck again.

We are all like Caesar's army. When luck is on our side,
we expect to do better, and so for the most part we do. Even
more, when luck is against us we expect to do badly; if our
best efforts are going to fail, what's the point in putting forth
our best efforts?

So luck affects almost everybody's life. Almost everybody
is conscious of it, and almost everybody tries to do something
to control it.

Mistletoe has run through all the shades of superstition. It is neither plant nor tree, neither one thing nor the other, outside recognised systems. Those who stand beneath its power make themselves free from conventions, but at the same time beyond the protection of conventions. So first it was an object of worship, like a God; then an uncanny, magical thing; then, among our prim great-grandparents, an excuse for kissing and being kissed when convention otherwise forbade. Now, from force of habit, we buy some at Christmas, hang it up, forget about it, take it down and put it on the bonfire.

CONTROLLING LUCK

The usual name for this is superstition. Hitler's lucky number was seven, and his lucky day was the seventh. During the second World War, when enormous amounts of supplies and vast bodies of men had to be moved about, he deliberately interfered with their movements so that his invading armies should cross the frontiers of the countries he was attacking on the seventh day of the month.

I don't know many millionaires, but I do know one who made most of his money manufacturing glass. He's a very successful and hard-headed businessman. When he gets up in the morning he always puts his left sock on before his right sock. So that he will know which is which, his wife sews a coloured stitch into one of every new pair of socks he buys.

Nehru, the great Prime Minister of India, wrote several letters to insist that a proper horoscope was made by a professional astrologer for his first grandson.

There is a goal-keeper in the First Division of the English Football League who invariably comes on to the field carrying a small parcel which he places in the back of the net. Only he knows what's in the parcel.

Colonel Fotherpottle: Aaaaaaaaaaaaaaaaaaaaaahhhhh— tishoooo!!!! Mrs Fotherpottle: Bless you!

Where does superstition begin? With Mrs Fotherpottle's little politeness? The Colonel sneezes about forty times a day, and Mrs Fotherpottle answers the same way every time. It's almost the only conversation they have. Surely Mrs Fotherpottle seldom thinks as she makes her automatic response to the explosion that she is warding off an attack by the devil? That's just habit, not superstition.

And where does superstition end? When the bishop, gold-robed and sonorous, raises his arms before the altar and leads the massed believers into the ancient ritual, is that superstition? Atheists would say so.

But for my purposes a religion doesn't count as superstition. First, because superstition is mainly involved with luck, with the small ups and downs of earthly affairs, not with the struggle between good and evil and the damnation of souls. Second, because superstitions come piecemeal— they don't build up together into a coherent body of belief. In fact a great many superstitions are self-contradictory. The soldier who believes it's unlucky to light three cigarettes with one match very likely also believes that there is a single bullet somewhere with his name invisibly written on it, and that is the one that will get him. This bullet is his fate. If he believes in it, he believes that the future is already fixed, in which case there is no room for luck to act.

Superstitions make you actually do something that you wouldn't have done if you didn't believe in them. When you say, "It's been a good week so far—touch wood," it depends whether you say "touch wood" for politeness—so as not to seem to be boasting—or whether you actually believe, however slightly, that boasting about your luck will change it. In the latter case you are superstitious, in the former you are not.

Here are three rather longer examples of superstitious people. Paul is the only one who is truly superstitious in my sense. Ella is only playing at superstition—it is part of her personality—but if she isn't careful the play may become real. For Dong, on the other hand, it is all just as real as the real world. Although you could say that everything he believes is superstition, it isn't quite in the sense I'm talking about. But Paul lives in a world where reason is king, and thinks and acts most of the time as 'reasonably' as anyone else—only he has these other beliefs.

Ella

Ella is fifteen, bossy and intelligent, always very lively in company but privately afraid that she is really rather dull and plain. If you ask her friends, they'll tell you that she's terribly superstitious, and explain about the time when her desk fell over during a test because she was determined to write it all with her legs crossed and there wasn't quite room. And then the teacher noticed that she was wearing her jumper back to front and got furious . . . and in the end Ella did better than most of them in the test (no wonder, with all that distraction and uproar).

I've seen Ella walk under a ladder, but she'd never have done it if she'd known I was watching. In the same way she loves the horoscopes in newspapers and magazines, but she waits to read them till she's got a friend there to hear her scream, or giggle.

Last year, on April 24th which is St Mark's Eve, she tried the old Yorkshire charm of sprinkling a fine layer of ash across the hearth last thing at night. She'd read that if there was a foot-print there next morning, the person in the house whose foot fitted it would be the next to die. When the family came down to breakfast they found the old cat's footprints there, and sure enough it did die a couple of months later. Ella tells this story in a whispery voice now, but at the time she was the first to point out that the cat walked about at night, and was so old that it was going to die soon anyway.

When Ella's cronies fall in love she makes them dig up a bit of earth which their boy-friend has trodden on, put it in a pot and plant a daffodil bulb in it. If the bulb flowers, it means the boy will be true for ever. But she hasn't tried it herself because, she says, the idea of any of the boys she knows being true to her for ever is a real drag.

Sometimes Ella goes a bit too far. When she spat on her sister's wedding-dress everybody was furious with her, and she couldn't persuade them it wasn't jealousy but a very old bit of good-luck magic. (No one in the family thought it odd that her sister went to the altar with a glove-button undone, and didn't fasten it till the service was over.) Ella's mother gets angry when Ella buys a new dress for a party, doesn't enjoy herself and then never wears the dress again. Ella's father thinks that this is only Ella's way of demonstrating to her mother that she can do what she likes about her own clothes.

If someone at school wears green, it depends what Ella feels about her whether she says how unlucky it is. She never wears green herself—it's lucky it doesn't suit her.

Paul

Paul is an actor—mainly a comedian but good enough to get a few straight parts too. He really believes his superstitions, and acts on them. For instance he'd have to be very short of money before he took a part in *Macbeth* or any play with the word "Peacock" in the title. He has more than once refused to go on stage because his mascot, a very old teddy-bear with both eyes missing, has been lost. All his friends know his story how once when this happened the programme was re-arranged to allow Paul to search for his teddy and at the exact moment when he would have been on the stage a piece of scenery collapsed and broke the collar-bone of the singer who had taken his place, and ten minutes later he found teddy in the dustbin where some cleaner had thrown it. It's a pity that the story isn't quite true—the scenery did collapse, but not on the same day that teddy was thrown away. If you point this out to Paul he'll never speak to you again.

Most of Paul's superstitions are concerned with avoiding bad luck. He doesn't worry so much about bringing good

D

luck. In fact, when he has a stroke of good luck he doesn't think of it like that at all—he thinks it's something he's *deserved*. In a way this is natural. When you do a trick like Paul's—for instance, making a whole audience laugh simply by your manner of saying "Bai Jove!"—you know you are doing something over which you don't have complete rational control. At any moment you may lose the gift, and there won't be anything—anything everyday and practical—that you can do about it. It's all a matter of luck, and Paul's superstitions are a way of trying to control his luck.

Dong

Dong is a hunter. He lives in a village in a clearing in a tangled forest, and he believes that at least half the other people in his village are witches, only he's never sure who they are, so he has to treat them all as if they were. In a way this is worse than it would be to live in the nearest village, four miles along the mountain. Everybody there is a witch, so at least Dong would know where he stood.

Dong himself is not a witch, but he's the only person who knows that. The safest thing for him is to behave as though he were a very powerful witch, so that none of the other witches will care to have a go at him. It is for this reason that he wears three iguana bones in his hair, and each morning when he wakes immediately spits towards the rising sun. Of course his real name isn't Dong—he keeps his real name a complete secret and changes it once a month by whispering the new name into a crack in a special fig-tree in the forest, into which he has put his soul for safe-keeping; he has borrowed the fig-tree's soul so that now, if the fig tree suddenly withers, he'll know that somebody has been trying to bewitch him and has got the fig tree by mistake. He hasn't even told his wife about the tree—not that he is certain she's a witch, and even supposing she *were* a witch it wouldn't be all that bad. Everybody knows that women witches are rather feeble until they become very old and bent, when they acquire new powers. Then the safest thing is to eat them.

The curious thing is that if you took all Dong's beliefs away from him he would probably be dead in a month. It's not only that the jungle is a dangerous place, especially at night, containing bushes whose touch is always agonising and sometimes fatal (so Dong believes they are inhabited by demons). Also, if you went into his village you would find it astonishingly clean and sweet-smelling because the whole tribe believe that you must bury your dung, far away from your hut, in a secret place, in case a witch uses it to gain power over you. At certain seasons, too, they boil their water because that is when the ghosts of dead witches swim up the river and try to get into a live man's body. The result of these two customs is that Dong's tribe is surprisingly free of the common, killing tropical diseases, and quite a lot of the women do grow old enough for the men of the village to decide that it would be safest to eat them.

THE SHADOW OF THE GALLOWS

Whether we believe in them or not, it's quite natural that we should want to think that our superstitions have come down to us through many centuries; we even tend to invent origins for them that have no truth at all, or at least no proof. We argue that a superstition wouldn't have survived so long if it didn't work. We enjoy thinking of it as the remnant of an ancient secret wisdom, from a time when men were familiar with magic. We may even feel that there is something magical in the superstition itself, that makes it live on so.

Take walking under ladders—it feels wrong when you do it, so that you sometimes even duck or cringe a bit, and there really is also the faint chance that a workman might drop a bucket on you. That ought to be enough, but you'll hear people say that the origin of the superstition goes back to a dread of walking under the gallows. It may be so, and it certainly adds a tremor to the shadow of the rungs.

It is said to be unlucky to light three cigarettes from the same match, or from a lighter without stopping the flame and starting it again. This is mostly a soldier's belief, though one finds it elsewhere. I've seen two explanations.

In the first World War there were lulls in the bombardment, when the hideous pounding moved to some other part of the line, and the exhausted troops in the trenches could relax a bit. Then the chief menace was the enemy sniper and your own carelessness. You lit the first cigarette and his attention was caught by the flare of the match. You lit the second and he had you in his sights. You lit the third and the bullet was already singing towards the smoker's brain.

Second explanation: in southern Russia only the priest may light the altar-candles, of which there are three; it is sacrilege for a layman to do so. From this a belief grew among the local peasants that it was at least unlucky to light things in threes. Then, when the French and British armies visited the place a hundred and twenty years ago for the bleak and

pointless war of the Crimea, one of their few comforts was smoking, and they picked the local superstition up and transferred it to this.

You could combine the two theories by arguing that the second is the true origin and the first a practical use for the belief. I myself think that neither is likely to be right—the trench warfare one is much too pat and the Crimean one plain unlikely. The holiness of flame and the holiness of the number three are quite enough to make some such belief grow up, though it might equally well have been that it is *lucky* to be the third smoker.

Of course some beliefs are very old indeed. The lucky horse-shoe probably goes right back to the beginnings of the iron age, or at least to a time when up-to-date iron-users made contact with old-fashioned bronze users, to whom the new metal was a marvellous strange stuff. Fairies, they say, cannot abide iron. Were these fairies in fact the last of the bronze-age people, hiding in remote places, seeming when hunted to melt into the very hills? There's no knowing.

At least we can be sure there was a time when iron was still fairly scarce and the most likely piece one would pick up by chance would be a cast horse-shoe; and it would also look the right shape to hold a bit of luck. There is a Lincolnshire rhyme, to be spoken as the shoe is nailed in place (a mell is a hammer):

Father, Son and Holy Ghost,
Nail the Devil to this post.
With this mell I thrice do knock—
One for God
And one for Wod
And one for Lok.

That seems proof of ancientry, because, though the rhyme starts primly with the Christian Trinity it ends with the old Norse Gods Woden and Loki, who haven't been *officially* worshipped in those parts for a thousand years.

The Scapegoat

In Manchester a child who sees a hearse or an ambulance must clutch his collar tight until he sees a four-legged animal —a goat is best but a dog will do—and then let go of his collar and cast his arms towards the beast, opening his hands wide to throw the ill luck that way. The beast takes the ill luck and the child goes scot free.

The Old Testament contains this instruction:

And Aaron shall cast lots upon the two goats; one lot for the Lord, and the other for the scapegoat . . . and Aaron shall lay both his hands on the head of the live goat, and confess over him all the iniquities of the children of Israel, . . . putting them upon the head of the goat, and shall send him away by the hand of a fit man into the wilderness. And the goat shall bear upon him all their iniquities unto a land not inhabited.

In the Balkans, until a few years ago, it was still possible to see the visit of the Fascinating Bear to a village. He was a real bear, very shabby and mangy, probably owned by gipsies. When small, he had had his arms and chest-bones broken to make his hug weak and thus prevent him from being dangerous (this nasty practice is still normal with dancing bears). When he came, the villagers carried their sick out into the street and bargained with the gipsies about how much they should pay the bear to take the sicknesses out of the human patients and into himself; a good bear would look very woebegone, as though he were already full of people's ailments. When the haggling was over the gipsies played their bagpipes and the bear walked to and fro over the sick, groaning as he did so. The sick people shrieked beneath his weight, louder than the pipes. Then they were carried back into their houses, and sometimes they did get better. Only certain bears were able to do this trick. You couldn't cure people with any old bear.

Boasting

The following superstitions all have one thing in common:

It is dangerous to have your wedding photographs taken before the ceremony.

In the great fashion houses of Paris no dress ever has its last few stitches put in until it is bought and paid for.

It is lucky to wear patched clothes.

When the roof is put on to a new building, especially a tall one, the workers, owners and architects meet for a Topping-out, at which they drink a toast of beer to the building and pour some on the roof.

Pride comes before a fall.

The peacock is bird of ill omen.

The gambler who touches a hunch-back's hump will have good fortune.

I'm not sure about the hunchback—perhaps there is another reason for this, or perhaps several (very few things happen for only one reason). But to touch a man is to show that you share a common humanity with him; so to touch somebody as obviously imperfect as a hunchback is to show that you are not proud, that you too are imperfect.

When Man makes such an obvious boast of his power as a skyscraper—such a challenge to the lightning bolt from the jealous powers—it is only sense to pour out a little sacrifice to them. In the Bible, Man's first communal sin—I mean the first thing men banded together to do, as opposed to such private sins as murdering one's brother—was to build a tower tall enough to provoke the anger of God, who cursed man for it with the curse of languages.

Pouring out a little beer seems a harmless and rather charming custom, especially when (as is sometimes done)

a little Christmas tree is raised on the roof too. But there was a time when the sacrifices were of a crueller sort. Ingenious people are always looking for the origin of nursery rhymes, usually with more daring than discretion. For instance, there's a neat theory that *Ring a ring of roses* is about the Black Death; the pustules caused by the disease are supposed to have been shaped like a rose, the posies were primitive herbal disinfectants, the disease caused sneezing, then the staggers, then collapse. It's very sad that Mr and Mrs Opie, those great authorities on Nursery Rhymes, believe that there's no evidence at all for this.

But they do seem to think that *London Bridge is Falling Down* may go back to the old custom of making a human sacrifice and building the body into the foundations of the bridge, and mixing the mortar with blood, all to appease the jealous god of the river. In the song the bridge is falling down

D*

and various suggestions are made for materials to build it up with, none of which will do. Iron and steel will buckle and bend; silver and gold will be stolen away; but then

> Set a man to watch all night
> (Dance over my Lady Lea)
> Set a man to watch all night
> (With a gay lady.)

In some versions the man is given a pipe and bowl to help him keep awake. Workmen demolishing a very old bridge in Spain found a skeleton in the stonework with a flask and cup and plate beside it. And the game, or dance, that used to go with the song was one of those where a file of dancers moves under the arched arms of two players, and each dancer tries not to be the one who is caught when the arms come down at "Set a man to watch all night."

Usually the sacrifice must have been a slave-child, or a war-prisoner. But sometimes the 'watcher' must have been chosen by lot from among the children of ordinary people. So the innocent dance and pretty song are faint echoes of the hideous moment of choice, whispering to us still out of the dark past.

Apart from buildings and proud behaviour and fine clothes, the most obvious way of tempting Providence is to claim to know what is going to happen next. The future is in the hands of God, or of the gods, or of the lord of luck—it depends what you believe. To say "I shall be as happy tomorrow as I am today" or "In ten minutes I shall have married the man I love" or even " Things are going very well for me these days" (implying that they'll go on like that), all these are very dangerous forms of boasting. You mustn't count your chickens before they are hatched.

Even to plant a seed is to claim to foresee a time when it will bear you a harvest. The Roman Catholic Church fought for centuries against the old Celtic custom of the Beltane fire.

Leaping the bonfire in an Alsace village

Nowadays where it survives this is a pretty folklore custom, with a bonfire built in the village square and young couples in traditional costume jumping through the flames. There's probably even a souvenir stall where one can buy picture postcards of the ceremony, which takes place on the first of May.

Fifty years ago, in the wilder parts of Brittany, Ireland and Scotland, the fires were lit with a purpose; cattle were driven through them as a protection against witches and to ensure fertility. Young couples jumped the flames for the same reason. Special cakes were blackened in the embers and eaten. In a few places a man was chosen by lot, dressed in a tall black hat and made to undergo a mock sacrifice in the flames.

The more romantic Celtic scholars are quite convinced that this picturesque rite, the offering of man and beast and bread to the flames, goes back to the deepest roots of Celtic history, to long before they were driven westward to the fringes of Europe, and worshipped the God Baal. To him at the great spring festival they sacrificed these things, so that he should not be angry with them for daring to presume that without his help babies and calves would be born un-maimed or corn grow unblighted.

Fear of boasting was the first superstition and it will be the last. Even among a race of super-scientists, who know the causes of things, I think the star-captains coasting home from successful missions along the spaceways will guard their tongues from saying how well things have gone until the landing rockets have flared and faded and they themselves have come safely down the gangway, staggering under the forgotten gravity of earth.

LUCKS, DOOMS AND CURSES

Only a mile from where I live there's a large mound of flints by the roadside. All the village children will tell you that it was built a hundred years ago by an old gentleman who buried his favourite horse beneath it. The horse, they say, was shod with golden shoes, and the old gentleman put a curse on anybody who dug for the gold. So far nobody's risked it.

A good curse makes a good story. Sometimes it's just a doom put on a family, but usually it inheres in some object, like the green eye of the little yellow god which Mad Carew stole in the poem. Somebody has to desecrate something to get a good curse going—steal a sacred jewel, break into a pharoah's tomb, chance on a forbidden ritual—but then the innocent suffer with the guilty.

I suppose the Hope Diamond is the world's most famous curse-bearer. This fabulous stone, from its appearance in Europe, dogged its owners with financial ruin, murder, suicide and accident. Within the space of ten years, towards the end of the last century, it was owned by an American who went bankrupt, a Russian who was murdered, a Frenchman who killed himself, a Greek who went bankrupt and a Sultan who lost his throne. It's now in the Smithsonian Institute in Washington.

But I prefer a story that goes with another famous curse, that of Tutankhamen: on November 25th, 1922, the famous tomb was opened; the overseer of the dig took a quick glance, but the Earl of Carnarvon, who had financed the work, was the first man to break into that three-thousand-year privacy and truly stare at the sacred gold. Within six months he was dying in a Cairo hotel of pneumonia following the infection from a mosquito bite in the Valley of the Kings. His son, who had hurried from India to his bedside, later told serious historians that as the Earl died every light in Cairo had gone out, for no reasons that the City engineer could discover.

At the same instant, far off in England, the Earl's favourite dog howled and fell dead.

Two other members of the archaeological team died nearly as soon; but the Valley of the Kings is an unhealthy place, and it was a large team, several of whom lived and worked into their eighties.

Here are another two examples of luck, good or ill, staying with a particular object or in a single family. Of course there are several different versions of each story: I've chosen the one which makes the best reading—which may not be the one scholars think closest to the truth.

The Luck of Edenhall

In the Islamic Art Room of the Victoria and Albert Museum there is a case containing several glass objects and a few silver ones. Among them is a yellow glass beaker, about six inches high, patterned with coloured enamel looking like the sort of unusable flower vase you find at the back of old aunts' china-cupboards. All the pictures of it make it look hideous. But if you stare at it you begin to see that it has great purity of shape, and that the enamel brings out a faint glow from the inside of the glass. Somehow it sings in the eye.

This is its story.

The Musgrave family became owners of Edenhall five hundred years ago. Not long after they came into possession of the house, the family butler went early one midsummer morning to draw water from St Cuthbert's Spring nearby. He walked so silently through the dew-soft grass that he surprised a party of the Little People sitting round the spring, feasting on the water as though it were wine. At the sight of him they leaped up and faded into the bank behind the spring, but when he reached the water he found by its side a strange goblet of yellowish brown glass, enamelled with rich red, pale green and milky blue. As he picked it up he heard a voice, faint but very clear, chanting

If this Cup should break or fall,
Farewell the Luck of Edenhall.

He carried it home and told his master the story, and from then on it was carefully treasured. In 1721 the wicked Duke of Wharton visited Edenhall, and one night there was a great drinking-match at which the men all drank toasts from the Luck. The Duke was in such rampageous spirits that when he had drained his toast he tossed the Luck high in the air. However, the Musgrave family seem to have been blessed with canny butlers, and this one had been waiting for some such frolic and caught the Luck in his napkin as it fell.

After that, whenever it was brought out, a servant stood by with a napkin ready to catch it. So it is still in perfect condition, standing in its case beside a fat blue-and-white bottle which bears the legend "Glory to our Lord the Sultan, the Wise, Just, Warrior King".

A more probable story is that the Luck was brought from Syria by a Crusader and became a token of tenure—when few men could read or write it was common for a great lord to give some object to one of his underlords, to show that he held such-and-such lands. So whoever owned the Luck owned Edenhall. This would account for the beginnings of the legend.

The Luck has been in the Museum for fifty years. Edenhall itself was pulled down during the second World War and the family live elsewhere. I haven't had the impertinence to write and ask them how their luck holds.

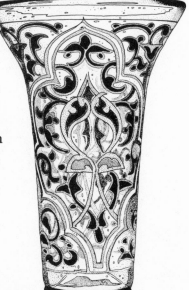

The Curse of the M'Alisters

In the bloody history of the Scottish clans many a mother or widow must have cursed men for the death of her sons or husband. A lot of these curses are said to have come true.

The Chief M'Alister More was no crueller than his kind, which means he was cruel enough. There was a widow of another clan who had two sons, and when M'Alister More made a sudden cattle-raid on that clan, he hanged them from the beams of their house, in front of their mother's eyes.

As he turned away, grinning, she shrieked, "M'Alister More, you have taken my sons from me. Be this on you! Never more shall a son be born in your house, until he that shall ride home at midnight to his bride."

M'Alister More laughed, and strode off to see to the driving of the stolen cattle. But for several generations only daughters were born to the clan chiefs.

Then, somewhere about 1690 a son was born and it seemed that the Curse had lifted. The boy grew up, and married, but soon after the wedding the Scots rebellion of 1715 began. Old M'Alister wanted no part of it, but young M'Alister kissed his wife goodbye and rode off to join the Earl of Mar who was fighting to put the Stuarts back on the throne. No news came, and no news came, and then at last a rumour that Mar had thrashed the English in a battle and James was King again.

The wife lay late awake. About midnight she heard hoofbeats on the hillside, and a moment later hoofbeats in the courtyard. Then footsteps on the stairs, and then the door creaking open. And there stood young M'Alister, in a soldier's uniform, his face white as paper and his head lolling on his shoulder as no living man's could.

The wife screamed and fainted. The servants who rushed to her aid found no one but her in her room, but in the courtyard they found young M'Alister's horse, dead, with the lather of sweat still drying on it. Next morning news came that the rumour of victory was lies, that young M'Alister had been captured at the indecisive battle of Sherriffmuir and hanged for a traitor.

CHARMS, AMULETS, TALISMANS

A stone with a hole in it, a silver model of an old shoe, another of a human hand, a horse-shoe, a foreign coin, a loose tooth, a glass locket containing hair, a ring, a pink felt mouse, a silver saint . . .

The list could go on for pages. They're all *charms*. Some of them may be *amulets*, which are charms to protect the wearer against magical attacks. Only the coin and the saint might be *talismans*, which are charms that work a single magical trick. The famous Lee Penny was a talisman, and was said to cure rabies, bleeding and cattle murrain. When the City of Newcastle borrowed the Lee Penny to fight a plague they paid the owners a bond of £6,000 as surety for its safe return.

The shoe might be the old shoe you throw out of the door as a friend sets out on a journey. He mustn't see you doing it, or he will lose the luck it brings. The hand might be a saint's relic, or just possibly a faint memory of that awesome object The Hand of Glory, which was made mainly from a murderer's hand hacked off as he swung at the gibbet, and was used to open locked doors.

The devil is strangely attracted by glass, and if the glass contains the hair of a saintly woman he becomes entangled in it and can work no harm. So the problem is to find a saintly woman. One's mother's hair is said to be an adequate substitute.

A stone with a hole in it? Some people can see visions through these. Kenneth Mackenzie, the Warlock of the Glen, owned such a stone. His end came when proud old Lady Seaforth sent for him to ask why Lord Seaforth was so delayed in Paris. He looked through his stone and bellowed with laughter, but refused to tell her what he had seen. She ordered her servants to build a rough gallows and string him up; then the Warlock, with the rope round his neck, confessed that he had seen Lord Seaforth sitting in a tavern with a girl

*All teeth are objects of occult powers. I have seen a whole fat book
devoted to the magical use of the tooth. A murderer's tooth was
especially potent, so much so that Goya's would-be witch was
prepared to risk the plague to get one.*

on his knee and another fondling his grey hairs. Lady Seaforth was so outraged that she hanged the Warlock anyway—but not before he'd put the Doom of the Seaforths on her family.

A ring is a symbol of perfection. An iron ring is said to cure the cramps in bed.

A pink felt mouse? I don't know, but it doesn't matter. The function of a charm is to be a house for your luck to live in, a small personal totem. If Sarah decides that her lucky object is the third stair up in her home, that's fine, except that she can't carry it about with her. On the other hand it'll be difficult to lose.

LUCKY NUMBERS

Numbers are mysterious things. We know what two left feet are, and May 2nd, and our aunt who is twice as fat as our other aunt. But what is Two? No two answers agree.

But numbers are a product of the human mind, so humans in all times and places have tended to have much the same feelings about them. The odd numbers, for instance, seem to be more associated with mystery than the even numbers. One is the number for God, three a holy number, five the number of man's soul, seven a magical number, nine doubly holy, thirteen unlucky. But two is the number for reason, four for justice, six for loyalty, eight for fate; there are Ten Commandments and twelve men on a jury, and so on.

You have two lucky numbers: your birth number is found by adding the day, month and year of your birth together,

adding the digits of that number together, and then the digits of that second number, until you reach a single-figure number. Your name number is found by giving number values to the letters of your name, adding them together and adding the digits as before. Your birth number rules your fate and your name number is your lucky number. The usual table of values is this:

$$
\begin{aligned}
A J S &= 1 \\
B K T &= 2 \\
C L U &= 3 \\
D M V &= 4 \\
E N W &= 5 \\
F O X &= 6 \\
G P Y &= 7 \\
H Q Z &= 8 \\
I R &= 9
\end{aligned}
$$

So Peter Dickinson makes $7 + 5 + 2 + 5 + 9 + 4 + 9 + 3 + 2 + 9 + 5 + 1 + 6 + 5 = 72; 7 + 2 = 9$. So my name number is 9.

Thirteen

This is the famous unlucky number. Many people believe that it got its bad reputation because there were thirteen who sat down to the Last Supper, when Judas betrayed Christ. But there were also thirteen of the Norse Gods present when Loki tricked blind Hodur into throwing the dart that killed bright Baldur. And long before the time of Christ thirteen was a death number for the Romans. Poor thirteen, it seems unfair to blame it for not being strong, tidy, logical twelve. The added one has turned it into a shambling and unusable number, a number nobody needs, a scape-number.

666

In the Bible, in the book of *Revelation*, there is a description of the end of the world. Seven seals are broken and seven trumpets sounded, while a thoroughly uncomfortable time is had by all except God's chosen, and finally a great and marvellous beast is loosed upon the earth, who deceives men with false miracles and rules the world. The last verse of this chapter reads

> *Here is wisdom. Let him that hath understanding count the number of the beast: for it is the number of a man; and his number is Six hundred three score and six.*

I've seen several interpretations of this, including one which made it out to be Adolf Hitler and another which, after juggling with the atomic numbers of hydrogen and uranium, applies it to the H-bomb. But its best-known user was a strange and unlovely but interesting man named Aleister Crowley, who took part in the great magical revival of the last century, and called himself 'The Wickedest Man in the World' and 'Beast 666'. He died only about thirty years ago. In old age he seemed harmless, but his followers explained that he used to have great powers, until one night in Paris when he tried to raise the horned god, Pan. He took over a whole hotel for this purpose. Most of his disciples waited below, while he and one other performed their rites in an

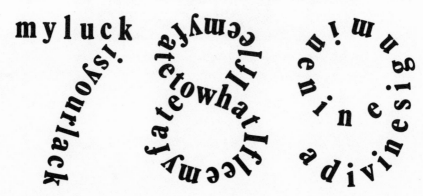

upper room. Those waiting heard cries from above, and the sounds of terrible struggle, but they were under strict instructions not to interfere till dawn. When they opened the room they found the other man dead, and Crowley huddled in a corner, gibbering. It took him four months to recover his sanity, and then his powers were gone.

Aleister Crowley in magical robes

GAMBLING

Two hundred years ago a gentleman was riding across a common not far from London. Now the place is all covered with neat rows of houses from which men go off every day to their offices, children to their schools and women to the shops, all knowing that today will be very much like yesterday.

But then it was a dreary upland, covered with gorse and sour grasses through which the autumn wind hissed like a man grooming a horse. The gentleman rode on, thinking philosophic thoughts, until he came to a more open space with a single large tree in the middle of it. Under the tree two men were sitting, and as the gentleman came nearer he saw that they were playing dice. Moreover they were as ragged a couple as he had ever seen.

They did not look up at the sound of his horse's hooves, but crouched over each throw as though their lives depended on the way the little cubes fell. The one who was about to throw shook the dice in his palm, crooked his fingers into a tube and blew down it, whispered a charm and at last rolled the dice across a patch of bare earth. Necks tense, the two heads craned. The man muttered and the other one picked up the dice.

"Good morning, friends," said the gentleman.

"Good morning, yer honour," said one of the men, barely looking up. But the gentleman was full of his philosophic thoughts, and also naturally inquisitive.

"You make a strange sight, sirs," he said, "sitting under this tree, in this wilderness, throwing dice. And you do not look as if you had many possessions to gamble with, apart from that rope."

At last the men looked up, gaunt-faced. One of them laughed.

"Yer honour is a man of grand observation," he said. "The truth is this—we are brothers, and we were born in

Ireland, and by the time we were men you could have told our name to any man in Connemara and he would have heard of it, for we were known through all that county for playing the dice, and no one had ever beat us. But Ireland is a poor country, so we settled to come to England to make our fortune. But we left our luck in Ireland . . ."

"It was crossing the sea took it," said the other man.

"Very like," said the first. "But as yer honour will have observed we did not make our fortunes. And nobody will play against a man who has no stake, for that man has nothing to lose. So we must play against each other."

"It is strange," mused the gentleman, "that you should still play so eagerly when you are so poor that nothing depends on the throw of the dice. I thought, as I rode up, that it was a matter of life or death."

They stared at him. Hunger or surprise made their eyes huge. This time they both laughed.

"I remarked that yer honour was a man of grand observation," said the first. "A matter of life or death it is, for we have been throwing the dice to decide which of us shall hang the other one."

He laid one hand on the rope and pointed with the other at the sturdy branch above his head.

"A grand stake is a man's life," said the second one in a dreamy voice.

The philosophic gentleman put his hand into his pocket and threw down enough small coins to buy them bread for several days. They thanked him in abstracted tones, gathered the coins into two equal piles and settled again to their dice. Soon they were too absorbed to hear the gentleman's farewell, so he rode on, his thoughts more philosophical than ever.

That evening, at his club, he watched a young lord stake his wife's whole fortune on a single rubber of picquet and lose, smiling.

The Mad Gamblers

Some of the world's craziest betting took place in the London Clubs in the eighteenth century, especially at White's, Almack's and Boodle's. Here are a few true stories from those days.

Lord Stavordale had lost £11,000 at White's in one evening, but in one hand of Hazard (a dice game, forerunner of craps) he won the whole sum back. To the other players' surprise he began cursing his luck. They asked why. "Now, if I had been playing deep," he said, "I might have made millions."

A gentleman was walking past White's when he staggered and fell, evidently with some kind of heart-attack. Passers-by ran for help, but when the doctor came the members of White's ran out and barred his way, saying that they had taken bets on whether the sick man would live or die, and the presence of a doctor would spoil the odds.

Once £180,000 was bet on a single throw at Hazard.

Another member bet £1,000 that a man could live for twelve hours under water. He found a desperate fellow, put him in a boat and sank it (presumably hoping that air-pockets would exist in which the man could breathe). However he lost both boat and man. Unabashed he made the same bet again.

Lord Alvanley bet £3,000 on a race between two raindrops.

Lord Cobham (a famously mean peer) bet one guinea that he could spit into Lord Hervey's hat and not apologise. (Lord Hervey was famously effeminate.) However, Lord C had mis-judged his man, had to apologise abjectly, and lost his guinea.

The Duke of Portland made £200,000 by gambling. His secret was that he ate nothing but toast and drank nothing but water, while the other members ate and drank themselves silly.

At Almack's the most serious gamblers wore masks to conceal their emotions. Even the spectators were careful what they revealed. One night a member feigned sleep all evening until he knew who the heaviest winner was likely to be. Then he left early and, disguising himself as a footpad, robbed the winner on his way home across the Park. Returning to the club he gambled the whole lot away before dawn.

Six Types

Psychologists have produced a lot of different explanations why people gamble. The trouble with psychologists is that they always try and find one explanation that explains everything. I think there are several distinct reasons for the madness, and a man may gamble for any one of them, or for two or three of them together.

Gambling is common among very poor people for the obvious reason. Consuelo lives in a South American slum on the outskirts of a big city. She has seven children, but her husband barely earns enough to keep three people properly fed, and some of that he spends on getting drunk every Tuesday night. Nevertheless every month he and Conseulo put on their best clothes and go to the lottery office and spend three days' wages on buying a share in a ticket in the state lottery. They have never won anything, but they know a man whose second cousin won a big prize five years ago. They are always talking about what they are going to do when their number comes up. Consuelo is going to buy an enormous candle for Santa Juanita, and she is going to go to Rome and kiss the Pope's hand, and she is going to buy a real brick house (not a tin one) with five rooms, and hire a woman to sweep the floors and a man to hoe the garden. Her husband is going to buy a new Chevrolet.

And in a way they are right. They and their children are almost starving already, so they can bear a little more starvation. To live as they have to live now is to live without hope. The lottery gives them hope, a dream-world which has a chance of coming true—a real chance, however slight. It gives them something to talk about, to argue over, to plan for. A reason for going on living.

(Their state, too, has a reason for running the lottery. It keeps Consuelo and her husband content with their impossible life. Take the lottery away and they might start trying to make their life possible in another fashion, and that's how revolutions begin.)

Diane speaks English with an American accent, but most people who know her imagine she's French. In fact she's Dutch. You might see her anywhere in the world that she can find two things—long, cloudless days and a gambling casino. She plays roulette, which is the game where a numbered wheel is spun and a ball is thrown on to it while it's still spinning, and when it comes to rest the ball lies on one of the numbers, from 0 to 36. The players bet on which number it will land on. Diane's number is always 34.

She goes to the casino every evening. Some nights she does not bet at all. Some nights she rather listlessly joins a

game and bets small sums of money on whether the number will be odd or even—that way she is part of the game and can get the feel of it without losing (or winning) much. But some nights she 'knows' belong to her and then she bets not just everything she can afford but everything she owns or can borrow. More than once she has lost all her money, has pawned her diamond earrings and brooch, and with the last of the money from that has begun to win. Every time 34 comes up the casino pays her thirty-six times her bet, so if it happens once in a dozen spins of the wheel—say once an hour—she is winning heavily, enormously.

She has done that quite often. But equally often her 'knowing' has been wrong and she has lost everything, and had to go to work in the hotel kitchens to pay for her stay. But that isn't important to her. Even having a huge sum of money in her purse after a great session isn't important to her. What *is* important is 'knowing'—the nights when she can feel the tide of luck surging through her like an electric current and the counters on the green baize blaze with colours so fierce that they don't seem part of this world at all. Those nights give her life meaning and purpose, so she doesn't grudge the seasons when she has to take a menial job— a waitress, perhaps—provided that outside the restaurant windows she can see cloudless days, and nights when the casino lights glitter across the bay.

Captain Dick is a professional gambler. He bets on horses. He is always smartly dressed and drives a fast sports car. Like Diane he has won and lost huge sums of money—in one week as much as most men earn in a lifetime—but he has always won more than he has lost. Because, unlike Diane, he wouldn't dream of betting a penny on 'knowing'. He likes to know, without the quotation marks. Of course he can't know that Red Admiral is *certain* to win the 2.30, but he can know that Red Admiral is a bit better than other people reckon, or that Precious Bane, the favourite, is past her peak—things like that.

He knows these things by hard work, listening for hours to boring men on the off chance that they'll let something slip, doing favours to friends in the hope that one day the favour will be returned by a hint about some horse, studying form, studying breeding, studying odds. (He was a dunce at mathematics at school, but now he's an expert in this particular sort of sum.) And at the end he knows that Red Admiral has one chance in four of winning the 2.30, and that he can lay a bet with a bookmaker who thinks that Red Admiral has only one chance in six—so he bets £10,000 on Red Admiral.

And three times out of four Red Admiral will lose—so that's £30,000 down the drain. But the fourth time Captain Dick wins £60,000. In England you don't pay income tax

on betting wins, either, so that only has to happen a couple of times a year for Captain Dick to be better off than the head of the biggest firm in Britain. That's why, though you see Captain Dick at every worthwhile race meeting, you practically never see him bet.

Upton Driver has a steady job in a biggish American city. He is a little below average height and a little above average girth. He is keen on baseball and football—keen on watching them on TV, that is. He never takes any exercise, and smokes too much. He owns two or three guns, which he cleans often but never uses. His game is poker. Three nights a week he joins a game in a bachelor friend's house and plays till four in the morning. Sometimes he wins quite heavily, but over the year he's a steady loser, because he doesn't see the game as a mathematical exercise but as a psychic power struggle. It's as though he carries an invisible totem about with him, and each time he wins a pot (especially if he does it by outfacing or bluffing one of the other men) he proves that his totem is stronger, and he himself more of a man. He hates playing against women. And even when he pays up at the end of a losing session, he likes to do so with a wise-crack, like they did in the gambling saloons on the old frontiers, when men were really men.

Nikos is a very happy gambler, because he is a mean millionaire.
He hates to lose even half a dollar, but to get up from the
tables twenty dollars richer is for him a true delight. On the
whole he wins as much as he loses, getting a tremendous
kick of excitement out of it each time, but there is one small
peculiarity. He isn't married, but he usually has a very pretty
girl around, and if she's a gambler and manages to coax
some stake-money out of the old ape, then she is quite likely
to win heavily. This is just one of those anti-statistical freaks
which happen to some people, as though Nikos's money itself
brought the girl luck. Nikos, sweating and trembling at the
low-stake table, will hear the buzz of drama from the other
room; after a bit he will get up and lumber through to
see what's going on (he's as inquisitive as a bear); there his
girl will be sitting, with a pyramid of won chips in front of her,
and at his coming she will leap to her feet and kiss him on
both cheeks and tell him he's beautiful and sit down to shove
the maximum possible stake out on to the table; and Nikos
will lay his hand on her head like a priest blessing a child and
lumber back to sweat and tremble at the low-stake table.

The only trouble is that sometimes the girl wins so much
that she can afford to leave Nikos and set up with a handsome
young artist. But apart from that he's the happiest gambler
I know. Only he doesn't know it.

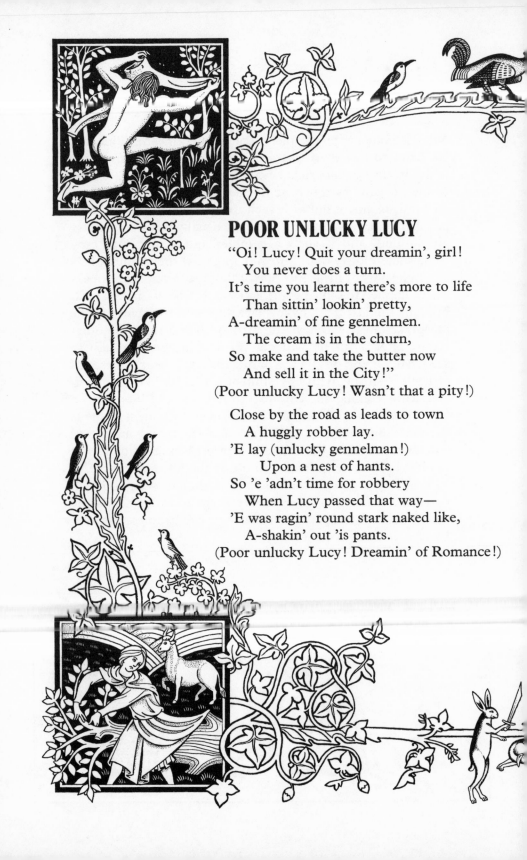

POOR UNLUCKY LUCY

"Oi! Lucy! Quit your dreamin', girl!
   You never does a turn.
It's time you learnt there's more to life
   Than sittin' lookin' pretty,
A-dreamin' of fine gennelmen.
   The cream is in the churn,
So make and take the butter now
   And sell it in the City!"
(Poor unlucky Lucy! Wasn't that a pity!)

Close by the road as leads to town
   A huggly robber lay.
'E lay (unlucky gennelman!)
   Upon a nest of hants.
So 'e 'adn't time for robbery
   When Lucy passed that way—
'E was ragin' round stark naked like,
   A-shakin' out 'is pants.
(Poor unlucky Lucy! Dreamin' of Romance!)

While Lucy stopped to gaze upon
   This hinterestin' sight
CRASH! in the road a'ead of 'er
   A rotten ellum dropped
(A wicked tree old ellum be
   And chancy with it) right
Upon the spot where Lucy might
   Of been—unless she'd stopped!
(Poor unlucky Lucy! Nearly she was copped!)

In climbin' through this hobstacle
   'Er cotton skirt she tore,
Hexposin' of 'er petticoat,
   A gracious shade of red.
And there was Farmer Boothroyd's bull!
   And red it was 'e saw!
'E pawed the ground! 'E broke 'is rope!
   'E charged! 'Ow Lucy fled!
(Poor unlucky Lucy! Now she's good as dead!)

She fled as quick as winkin' to
    The bridge acrost the river
And the bull come quick be'ind 'er
    And 'e was of monstrous weight.
When 'e stamped upon the timber, why,
    The bridge begun to quiver,
And it broke! And they fell through it!
    And the river was in spate!
(Poor unlucky Lucy! What a 'idjus fate!)

The bull falls in the water, like,
    But Lucy in a boat,
For 'ere comes this fine young gennelman
    A-puntin' on the stream
When down into 'is arms there falls
    A crimson petticoat
Containin' one young lady what's
    As pretty as a dream!
(Poor unlucky Lucy! If you'd 'eard 'er scream!)

"Ow, Lady in red petticoats,
   Now will you be my bride?
For never till this moment did
   My 'eart feel Cupid's sting!
I ham the Duke of Dumbleshire.
   My lands are rich and wide.
There'll be pearls upon your weddin' dress
   And di'monds in your ring!"
(Poor unlucky Lucy! 'Opin' for a King!)

You'll 'ave to tell yourselves the rest—
   My tale goes on for hours,
And just the same the 'ole way through
   'Cos Lucy's made that way.
'Owever full 'er life is of
   Hexcitement, wealth and flowers
She thinks about what might of been
   And sighs "Alackaday!"
(Poor unlucky Lucy! Only 'uman clay!)

MAGIC & WITCHCRAFT

a cat walking backwards
a column of cold still air in a warm room
a tree growing out of a chimney
a flare of light on the midnight hill-top
a voice, inside your head, saying your name
drums

The entrance to the cave seems to throb and waver. Now it is just a square opening, through which the priestess can see a sun-browned mountainside and part of the roof of a temple, and now it is a misty screen out of which dark shapes of men appear to ask her questions. The seeping gases from the crack at her feet fill her brain and make her so dizzy that she would fall if she weren't harnessed to a three-legged structure, gilded and jewelled but strong enough to steady her.

The priests by the entrance stir; three strangers are there, with a gift for the God which they place on the stone slab on the left before advancing into the middle of the cave. They look well-dressed and confident and the priests receive them with respect. One stands forward to ask his question.

"Servant of the God, our city is troubled. Three times in the last year have sentries been killed by lightning on the walls, as they stood guard with their iron spears in their hands. Is this mere chance, or is it a sign of anger from some God?"

The priestess leans forward in her harness to draw a deep breath of the gases from the crack. At once the cave becomes a vague, swaying place. Her lips froth. She moans and bubbles, a series of meaningless noises. By the time she recovers the priests have taken the delegation aside and interpreted the noises into words.

The next shape at the entrance is an old woman, who offers the God the least possible gift—one bronze coin and a loaf of bread—before darting into the middle of the floor and crying, "God, please God, give me a lucky day for my son's wedding. He's a good son, and . . . and . . ." She stops and stands trembling. The priestess merely sniffs at the gases and begins to mumble, like somebody very drunk, the first words that come into her mind, part of a lullaby her own mother used to sing. A young priest leads the old woman away to explain what this may mean.

The priestess waits. She has nearly done her two hours and then it will be Helen's turn to sway in the harness and breathe the fumes. From the attitude of the priests she guesses that the next questioner is somebody of importance. A shape looms at the entrance, a young man . . . but before he has placed his gift on the slab, before she can lean into the warm gases, the cave vanishes. She feels every muscle lock rigid. From far behind her, infinitely far, she feels the energies of the God rushing in, focussing, tearing through the narrow channel of her throat. Overwhelmed by the pressure of His presence she does not hear His voice speaking through her lips, telling the young man in one clear and unmistakable sentence his frightful destiny.

MAGIC IS...

. . . a way of coping with the erratic whims of chance.
. . . a way of seeking for luck.
. . . a way of looking forward into the misty paths of destiny.

Chance first. In the advanced and 'civilised' world we have a system for dealing with chance, for explaining its behaviour and then for seeing that it works to our advantage. We call this system Science.

Our ancestors and primitive peoples had and have a very similar system, which is called Magic. In fact much of modern science grew out of magic, by way of alchemy and astrology; and some anthropologists argue that magic is really science too. Plenty of things that pass for science are next door to magic, just as the space-warp with which the star-captains in SF stories leap across the light-years is next door to seven league boots. Many psychiatrists would claim that the extraordinary effects which some witch-doctors achieve come from an instinctive understanding of the science of psychiatry; few would admit that they themselves have a good fundamental grasp of witch-doctoring.

Where chance rubs hardest magic is most believed in. In many countries, even now, there is a moment at funerals when a curse is laid on the witch who caused this particular death. The mourners know that all men must die, but they still ask why Thomas Mpangwe? Why now? Who has caused this death? They cannot accept that death is a lottery— and in countries where two out of every five babies die before they can walk, death is a hard lottery to accept.

The Magic in Luck and Destiny is easier to see. The gambler who takes the bone of a frog's leg to the horse-races and the diner who throws spilt salt over his left shoulder are both using small magics, one to bring good luck and the other to ward off bad. The gipsy at the fairground who tells fortunes with the Tarot Cards and the Finance Minister who consults his wife's astrologer before bringing in a new budget are both using great magics, in an effort to see into the future. But the Magic of Chance is easily the most widespread.

This is the pattern, all the world over. Things go wrong, and no one is obviously to blame: but something must be causing the rust in the wheat, the lightning in the thatch, the plague in the army—something unearthly, a secret enemy, a witch. So the answer is to employ an expert in such matters (usually called a witch-doctor and usually also a witch) to find out the secret enemy.

Tarot cards are a respectable form of magic for seeing the future

A WEST AFRICAN WONDER-WORKER

He lives in the dark, far from any village. Only one special priest in the village knows the path to his hut; and though villagers are quite often taken there, when they come back to their village they forget the path, even though they may be hunters who know all the district round the village. In fact such hunters unconsciously avoid the area of the wonder-worker's hut; it is as though there were a gap in their mental maps of their hunting-ground. Suppose a hunter wounds a wild hog which runs bleeding towards the wonder-worker's hut; the hunter will follow the blood trail, but at a certain point, however plain it seems, he will lose it, curse his luck and go after other game.

When a villager wishes to consult the wonder-worker, he pays the priest to purify him and lead him to the hut. The journey is a quite ordinary one, by daylight. Perhaps at certain points the priest may perform a small ceremony—burn a few scented leaves—but that is all. After a couple of miles they leave the path and move off into the bush, which is a mixture of scrub and coarse grass and rock outcrops, with occasional small stands of taller trees, all looking so alike that it is very easy to get lost. After another mile they reach a thicket into which they crawl along a narrow tunnel through the tangled branches. Inside the thicket is a small clearing, containing the wonder-worker's hut, which is built so low that its thatch touches the ground. Again the only way into it is a narrow tunnel.

The priest tells the villager to wait while he crawls into the hut to prepare the wonder-worker. This is most necessary, as the wonder-worker lives in a permanent state of trance and can neither feed himself nor clean himself. When he is not being used by the priest he sits completely motionless, all the time, with a pulse beating at half the human rate and breathing slower than sleep. The villager waits in the silence,

becoming steadily more afraid.

At last the priest crawls out and gives the villager a tom-tom to beat. He himself kneels by the entrance and starts to shake a little rattle, calling all the time to the spirit in the wonder-worker to show himself. It may take twenty minutes before the steady tonk of the tom-tom and the dizzy sound of the rattle and the wail of the priest's prayers draw the wonder-worker from his trance.

Suddenly a face shows at the entrance—no human face, but a mask, carved and daubed with white clay. Instantly the priest kills, in a hideously cruel fashion, a cockerel he has brought with him and lets a drop of blood fall on to the mask. The wonder-worker wriggles into the open and crouches while the priest drops more blood on to his feet.

Then the wonder-worker begins to dance.

It is a dance of appalling energy, done in a half-crouch with every muscle straining with the power of the spirit inside. A normal, fit man who tried to dance like that would fall down exhausted in five minutes, but a wonder-worker can keep it up for an hour, provided the tom-tom goes on beating. The moment that sound stops he stops also, as if a film had stuck in the projector.

Probably the villager has come to ask about something that has gone wrong. What fetish has been offended that makes his son lie groaning all day in the hut? Why is his nut-tree dying? Why is his new cow barren?

The priest chants the questions, saying the same words over and over again while the wonder-worker jerks to the beat of the tom-tom. Then the wonder-worker answers in the high, tearing shriek of the spirit inside him, speaking in the spirit language which the priest alone can interpret. The boy has offended a strong ghost by throwing stones into a termite nest which the ghost uses as a house. The villager has done a bad thing by not taking enough beer to the funeral of his mother's brother. A witch has put a spell on the cow because the villager's wife refused to give her meat when she begged for it. In the first two cases new sacrifices must be made, but in the third a witch finding will be held, with all the suspects present; if the priest and the wonder-worker are skilled at their job they will find a witch, somebody already unpopular in the village, whom everybody can accept as the culprit.

But that's in the future. Now, at a sign from the priest, the villager slows the beat of his tom-tom and allows the dance to quieten into a ghastly twitch. The priest takes the shuddering hands and leads the man to the hut entrance, where he purifies him with holy water and the blood of another cockerel before leading him back, still faintly jerking, into the long darkness of his trance.

NIGHTMARES AND OUTCASTS

A witch is a woman who wears a black, pointed hat, flies through the air on a broomstick, keeps a black cat who is her familiar, has a pact with the devil and prefers to do mischief.

A witch is a West Indian police chief who can turn himself into a cow.

A witch is a French Countess who keeps her skin beautiful by bathing in the blood of babies.

A witch is an old woman gathering dandelion leaves in a ditch.

A witch is an African villager who can afford to build a brick house because he has dead men working for him on a distant mountain.

A witch, in fact, is anyone whom the neighbours believe to be a witch, anyone who believes herself (or himself) to be a witch, and any imaginary person round whom people's joint nightmares gather.

(I am not counting the modern witches to whom witchcraft is a form of nature-worship. They call themselves witches, but I am not using the word in that sense.)

However various witches may be, they can be divided into two sorts—the Nightmares and the Outcasts.

The Nightmares are the sort you mostly read about—they are the Secret Enemies. They deny, reverse or undo the things that a particular society thinks good or important. Among peoples where there is one God, and His Word is light, the witches meet in the dark to worship the devil. Among peoples where property and inheritance are important, they damage farms and change children. Among peoples who have strict and elaborate rules about who may marry whom, they creep into huts by night, and into beds, and flout these rules. Among sexually strict peoples they are wanton. And so on.

Some of the things they do are simply denials of what makes

man man. In Central Africa you can often tell a witch by his habit of hanging upside down from trees, and calling for salt when he is thirsty.

The Outcasts are the real witches. Almost all the men and women in history who have been tried and burnt or hanged for witchcraft have been Outcasts, though at their trials bits of the Nightmare have been produced as evidence. When things go wrong in a village—cattle fall sick, or rains rot the harvest, or children die—there is a tendency to look for a single cause, someone to blame. Where the real causes of things are not understood, this will usually be a person whom the community has already in some way rejected, or whose loss will not matter. Women live longer than men, so in such

An English witch-hanging from a political pamphlet of 1655.

villages there is nearly always some old widow, living alone, with cats for company, so poor that she has to gather strange wild plants for food, so lonely that she talks to herself or her cats, and perhaps a bit crazed too.

Suppose Farmer Elkins has a favourite cow which strays into Mrs Redditch's garden and eats a row of young peas. He is coming down the lane to look for his cow when he sees Mrs Redditch driving her out of her garden with shrieks and curses. He is afraid of Mrs Redditch—she has often been seen picking curious herbs out of the hedgerows, and Farmer Bellow's wife saw her walking round the four-acre just before all the wheat in that field was struck with a blight.

So either Farmer Elkins will do his best to appease Mrs Redditch—take her half a ham, perhaps (almost the only protein the poor old hag has seen for a year); or he will take the cow home and try to ward off the effect of the curses, by drenching the cow with holy water, or asking another witch for potions, as a result of which the cow will quite likely fall sick. And even if she doesn't, Farmer Elkins's nerves will probably affect the animal until she gives less milk.

Either way Mrs Redditch has had an effect, has changed the Farmer's life. She has used power. This is what witchcraft is about. And even if Mrs Redditch isn't a member of the local coven, after a bit of treatment like this she'll probably begin to believe that she *can* blight corn and sicken cattle.

THE COVEN

The word simply means 'meeting', and comes from the same root as 'convent' and 'Covent Garden'. It is pronounced *cuvven*—though occasionally on radio or TV you will hear some modern witch pronouncing the first syllable to rhyme with 'rove'.

Modern Western witches do very little cursing and spell-binding. Their chief activity is gathering into groups of thirteen and getting into communion with nature by dancing around naked. They claim to be perpetuating a religion that is older than Christianity—as old, perhaps, as the first true farmers in the world—the religion of the horned god whose favour allowed the crops to grow and whose anger blighted field and fold.

I don't know why the god is horned—perhaps to represent the creatures of the wild from whom the farmer took his land to sow his crops, and whose anger had to be appeased—but it is easy to see why the religion might have lived on even when other official religions seemed to have a complete hold on

the people. It took place at the peasant level, in secret, and
so was no challenge to the big organised churches. And
especially under mediaeval and puritan Christianity—which
was anti-sex and anti-woman—a cult which was pro-sex
and pro-woman must have had a lot of appeal.

And it mustn't be forgotten that life in remote districts in
the old days was a mixture of slogging hard work and boredom;
so there would be every temptation to join in the wild,
forbidden frolics on the midnight heath.

The evidence at witch-trials makes a coven-meeting
sound more like a riotous party than a religious ritual. What
rites there were were almost games, such as leaping through
bonfires. The revels would centre round a horned figure,
a masked man dressed in skins. (If you weren't sure who he
was, you could more easily whip yourself into believing that
the Dark Master had truly come to your festival.) At the
climax of the rite he had sex with the women, usually miming
the act and not really performing it. Then they would all go

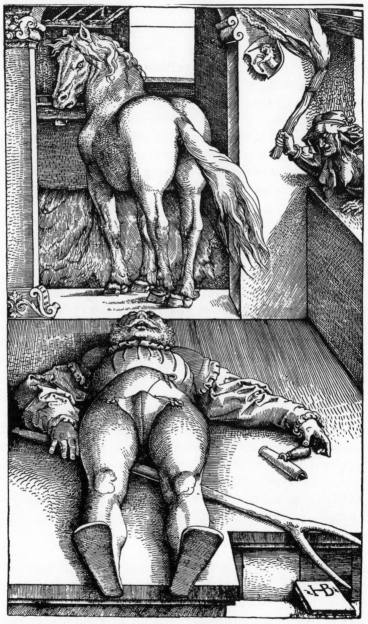

'The Groom and the Witch'. In contrast to the crude engravings in most witch-pamphlets, this German drawing seems to me to have a mysterious force. But nobody knows what it means, or what it refers to.

home, sleep soundly, and be ordinary men and women next day with barely a sly glance between neighbours to show that they knew more than Parson guessed.

That is one theory. Another theory is that there never were any covens, and that witches who confessed to joining one only did so because they knew what they were expected to say. Or they were poor crazed old things who actually believed they had been out on the heath when they had never left their homes.

I think there really were covens, though not everyone who confessed to belonging to one did so. Even if the coven wasn't the sad remains of an old religion, I think that once the idea had spread about there'd be people who'd give it a try. Some things sound crazy—for instance how could so many witches have persuaded themselves that they actually flew to the covens? Perhaps they were bullied and tricked into the confessions their accusers wanted, but another possible answer might lie in the famous flying ointment, which they were supposed to smear not on to their broomsticks but themselves.

The base for this ointment was the fat of a young child, but the active ingredient was usually belladonna or hemlock, both deadly poisons which, when absorbed in small quantities through the skin, might well produce strange sensations—in one case a swooning daze and in the other high excitement.

There is an amusing theory about these broomstick flights to covens. Before the witch went out, she put an elder log in her bed, with her night-cap on it. A small spell would make it assume her likeness. Then she cried "Horse and Hattock!" and whisked away to her midnight of madness. Next day she might well want to hint to a friend what she'd been up to, without letting anyone else into the secret, so she'd say "I slept like a log last night."

And that, they say, is the origin of that phrase. It seems a bit too neat to me.

It was a Nightmare that waited for travellers on the pass above the City.

In a land where men were masters, under a heaven ruled by the great male gods, she was a woman. Her eyes were dark gold, expressionless as a cat's under her smooth, calm forehead; her nose small and fine, her full lips soft and red, her neck blue-veined like marble. In a land of cities, walled and rich, she was the untamed wild. Her body was a lion's, stronger than a man. Her wings were an eagle's, swifter than a man. No traveller, not even a hero, could hope to fight or escape her. He could only stand there, hear her question, and then try to answer it while man's pride, his reasoning soul, shrank to nothing under her magical gaze.

What did she think, what did she dream, as she waited among the rocks? Nothing. She was a Monster, a creature formed to do her single nightmare deed. Until that sequence was triggered by a certain type of movement in the pass, she was inert, as dead as the rocks around her.

Time passed, days and nights. She did not notice. Then, one hot morning, a traveller came swinging along the white road over the plain, cocked his head to study its snaking rise to the ridge, took a fresh grip on his staff and started to climb. That action, the particular movement that a human's limbs make as he walks, triggered the sequence.

The Nightmare woke. She moistened her red lips. She waited to do her deed.

To cure bad eyes

For a boy with bad eyes, find a woman who has never seen her father. On nine days in succession, first thing in the morning, let her take a nettle leaf, make a small hole in it and blow through this hole into the blind boy's eyes. He will see.

For a girl with bad eyes a man who has never seen his mother must do the same.

If you find yourself surrounded by water-snakes

Cast among them three leaves of betony, and they will fall to fighting until all are dead.

To stop horses having nightmares

Give them pills compounded of garlic, liquorice and aniseed.

To heal a scald

Take nine bramble leaves. Dip them in spring water and apply them to the scald, saying the following charm three times for each leaf

There came three ladies from the east,
One with fire and two with frost.
Out with fire, in with frost.

To make three girls, or three gentlemen, appear in your room

For three days do no wickedness of any kind. On the fourth day, rise and clean your room well. Tell your servant that you are not to be disturbed all day. Eat no food. Take down all hanging objects—pictures, clothes, curtains, bird-cages and the like. Make sure the room is very clean and tidy. When that is all done, you may eat.

After supper go to your room and set out the table with a clean white cloth, three white wheaten rolls and three glasses of water. Put three chairs round the table and one at the side of the bed. Open the window. As you go to bed, say these words:

"Besticitum consolatio veni ad me vertat Creon, Creon, Creon, cantor laudem omnipotentis et non commentur. Stat superior carta bient laudem omviestra principiem da montem et inimicos meos o prostantis vobis et mihi dantes quo passium fieri sincisibus."

At that the three visitors will appear, sit in the chairs, eat drink and talk among themselves. If you are a man, it will be three girls; if a woman, three gentlemen. When they have finished their meal they will cast dice, and the winner will come to sit in the chair by your bed. You may ask any question, even about the finding of hidden treasure, and it will be plainly answered.

On the stroke of midnight all three will thank you and vanish; but they will leave behind a ring which, if you wear it, will bring you luck at gambling.

For good luck at games and work

Find a forked root of bryony, as like human shape as you can. On a Monday midnight, when Venus is in conjunction with the Moon, bury it in the churchyard. Water it with milk in which you have drowned three field-mice. A month later dig it up and it will be the exact likeness of a man. Bake it in an oven until it is hard, then wrap it in a dead man's shroud and keep it in a secret place. As long as no other person knows of it your luck will last.

To cause a horse to keep losing its shoe

Take three discs of Honesty, also called Moonwort, and bind them into the horse's tail.

To understand the voices of birds

On the Feast Day of Simon and Jude (October 28th) go into the wood with your dog and two friends and kill the first animal you see. Take it home, cook it in a little pot with the heart of a fox, and eat it. Then you will understand the speech of birds, and moreover any person you kiss will also understand it. But note, you must do your hunting in the right wood, and the spell for finding this is lost.

To choose the most faithful of four lovers

Pick four large thistle-heads. When you go to bed give each the name of one of the men you would choose between and place it at a corner of your pillow. If, by the morning, one has grown a fresh shoot, the man it was named for will be most true to you.

To stop dogs barking at you

Put a leaf of Hound's Tongue into the soles of your shoes.

For a girl to draw the man she loves to her

Sow the seed of hemp in nine furrows. As you sow each furrow, whisper

Hempseed I sow. Hempseed I sow
O young man that I love,
Come after me and mow.
  I sow. I sow.
Then, my own dear,
Come here, come here
   And mow. And mow.

ISOBEL GOWDIE

About three hundred years ago a pretty, red-headed Scots woman, the wife of a local farmer, was walking alone on the downs when a man dressed all in grey approached her and very directly asked her whether she would follow him. She understood him well enough, because there were several covens in the district. She was bored with her dull husband and dull life, so she said yes.

That night the two of them stole into Auldearne Kirk, where he baptised her into his religion and scratched her with the witchmark, to show she now belonged to him.

The coven she joined was attended by both men and women, the men with fairy names. Isobel was quite sure that they were demons out of hell, and that the man in grey was the Devil himself. When they met they danced and feasted and made love; but they also tried to use their weird powers to amuse themselves and to plague their enemies. Isobel said at her trial that she and the other witches could turn themselves into cats and hares, and that she owned a little horse to whom she could cry "Horse and Hattock in the Devil's name!" and he would fly with her to the meetings.

At her trial Isobel seemed perfectly sane. She gave her

These creatures from a medieval chronicle run the gamut from medical cases to demons

evidence against herself (for she was her own main accuser) clearly and soberly, even when she claimed that they had at one point been allowed into the hollow hills to meet the King and Queen of Faerie, and that the coven had at another time broken into the local dyeworks and bewitched it so that it could only dye the Devil's colour, black.

So far, so harmless. But she also said that she had killed a ploughman and a woman by flicking elf-bolts (the little chipped flint arrowheads of the stone-age people) at them. They made a clay baby and roasted it to kill all the children of a local landlord. They dug up the body of an unchristened child and used it magically to blight the crops of local farmers. They ploughed ground using toads to pull a little plough made out of a ramshorn for the same purpose. And so on.

And then Isobel became bored, even with those excitements. She wanted more, and she got it by going to the magistrates and confessing, of her own accord, what she had done. They questioned her several times, carefully, but her story remained the same. She didn't even (as hysterical confessers often do) keep adding new and more thrilling details. In the end she was hanged, and many of her coven with her, and their ashes scattered abroad.

A SCRAP OF PAPER

An old woman was brought to court in London, accused by her neighbours of witchcraft. They said she had a charm, strange writing on a piece of paper that had been given her many years before by a learned man. She had boasted of the power of this charm, and told how it had cured her daughter of a sickness that no doctor could remedy. And in quarrels she had threatened her neighbours with its power—which was unwise, because nobody minds how you cure your own daughter, but it's quite another thing to threaten neighbours with magical inscriptions. So she was arrested and brought before Chief Justice Holt.

The Chief Justice heard the evidence of accusation. He heard the prosecutor ask the old woman whether she was a witch.

"No, sir," she mumbled.

"Do you deny, woman, that you possess a paper inscribed with mystic words?"

They had to ask her several times. She was muddled in her wits, and though she didn't wish to be taken for a witch she could not go back, in front of the neighbours who crowded the court, on all her past boasts. In the end she fumbled under her clothes and produced a dingy cloth packet, which she unwrapped. She took out a bit of paper, yellow with age.

"Let me see this paper, usher," said the Chief Justice, and it was brought to him.

He peered at it a moment, smiling at the meaningless jumble of Latin Words. Then his eyes opened wide and he stared across the court at the prisoner.

"Tell me," he said, "did you at one time keep a lodging house in Fetter Lane?"

"I did, sir, and a very good house it was too, and a good neighbourhood. Not like . . ."

The Chief Justice held up a hand. The usher yelled for

silence. The old woman stood glaring at the crowd of her accusers.

"This is my own writing," said the Chief Justice. "When I was a student of law I lodged in this woman's house. I remember that she had a sick daughter. One winter, when I had no money to pay my rent, I persuaded her to take instead a charm to cure her daughter. I wrote some nonsense on a piece of paper and gave it her and she was satisfied. The women is no witch."

So he directed the jury to acquit, which they did. And later he habitually acquitted witches brought before him if he possibly could, and other judges began to copy him, so some good came of it all. But I doubt if the old woman was entirely pleased.

PERSECUTION

The case of the Scrap of Paper happened within a few years of Isobel Gowdie's trial in Scotland. About the same time a young woman came to court in England and confessed to the most grisly kinds of witchcraft. After hearing the evidence the judge ordered that she should be locked up, and a specially handsome jailor chosen for her. Within six months they were married; the girl forgot her practices (or fantasies) and became a sober citizen.

England had a surprisingly good record over the persecution of witnesses; the figures are hard to be sure of, but one good guess is that in the two hundred years of witch trials we burnt or hanged or drowned about a thousand men and women for witchcraft. In the rest of Europe, in a rather longer period, the figure may have been nearer a million. For instance one Polish judge called Benedict Carpzov is said, between 1620 and 1666, to have sentenced 20,000 people to death for sorcery.

This has little to do with the natural goodness of the

English. On the Continent it was normal practice to torture suspects to extract evidence. So an old woman in agony would scream out any names she could think of, friends and neighbours first, then local notables, saying that they were members of her coven, just to get the torturers to stop. So the terror spread to new suspects, high and low.

The best-known English witch-hunts took place in Essex towards the end of the reign of Elizabeth I. The authorities employed a witch-finder—what they called a 'cunning man'. Matthew Hopkins detected about thirty old women as witches in eighteen months; his system was to slide a pin into a suspect while her attention was elsewhere; if she felt no pain she was a witch. He would also look for the witch-mark, where the devil had scratched her to brand her for his own, and the extra nipple at which she fed her familiar with her blood. (Most people have areas on their bodies which contain very few pain nerves; any scratch will do for a witch-mark and any wart or pimple for a nipple; Matthew Hopkins was paid piece-work—so much money for every witch he found.)

Was Hopkins completely unscrupulous, ready to denounce anybody against whom an accusation might be believed, provided he received a fee? Even to ask the question is to look at the trials with twentieth-century eyes. Hopkins, and the people of Essex, including the accused themselves, all believed in the existence of witches; and with most of his mind Hopkins probably thought he was doing a service to society and deserved to be paid for it. There is even a little evidence that he retired from the job because he came to doubt the value of his methods.

The last witches to be killed in England died in 1751, fifteen years after the last official laws against witchcraft had been repealed. In the sleepy, straggling brick village of Long Marston in West Hertfordshire a crowd led by the local chimney-sweep burst into the work-house, dragged out an

17th-century engraving of Matthew Hopkins, two witches and their familiars

old man and his wife, stripped them naked, tied their thumbs crossways to their big toes, put ropes round them and dragged them to and fro through a duck-pond until they were dead. Later the chimney-sweep was arrested, tried and hanged for murder, a punishment which a lot of local people thought unfair. (We're usually taught that the official law lags behind public opinion, but here's one instance where it seems to have been ahead.)

It was extraordinary how long the old beliefs took to die in remote pockets. In 1894, when the first internal combustion engines were already running, only two years before Marconi sent his first wireless messages and nine years before the Wright Brothers got their first aeroplane off the ground, a small crowd gathered in Ireland to watch a young woman being burnt alive. Her father and husband were in the crowd. They believed that her body was occupied by a fairy or demon, which would be driven out by the fire.

The logs were lit, the woman died (suffocated, probably, by the smoke before she felt much pain). The flames roared and sank and the embers crumbled and became ashes. Then the crowd moved off to one of those strange stone-age camps, rigged with earth ramparts, that country people have always associated with the fairies, often believing that they contain a secret entrance to the fairy halls inside the hills. They waited, the dead woman's husband gripping a black-handled knife. Soon, they believed, she would appear before their eyes, whole and new and riding a white horse. Then the husband must leap forward and cut the reins with his black-handled knife, and she would become an ordinary human again.

They waited and waited. Nothing came.

DEVILS

Witches were not the only magical beings that could bring mischance and bad luck. According to one mediaeval expert there were also exactly 1,758,064,176 devils roaming the surface of the earth causing various kinds of trouble. Most of these had special duties. Here are a few whose names and arts can be found in no other book.

Ulambutor

Lived in fish-ponds and hung old sandals on fishermen's hooks. He was busiest in Lent.

Ognardo

Pestered farmers. When a man went to care for his bull, Ognardo would prance in front of him, invisible to the man but visible to the beast. The honest bull, with no malice at all in his heart towards his master, would charge at the foul imp, who would dodge at the last instant, leaving the farmer to be tossed high into the haystack.

Fanfan

Sat in chimneys and caused them to smoke. He also tried the tempers of cooks by making fires and ovens burn irregularly, so that feasts were served all burnt, or almost raw.

Ascuval

Lurked under bridges, smoothing the surface of the water so that pretty maids going to market might lean over to admire their reflections and thus fall into the sin of vanity.

Pollux

Pulled out the hairs of men, one by one, causing baldness and making his victims look ridiculous at a time when they ought to look wise and venerable.

Woodman

Was one of the surprising number of fiends allowed into churches, even on Sundays. He tickled men's noses, so that they sneezed during the sermon. Some say that he also caused snoring, but this cannot be true; for if a man be asleep during the sermon he is already sinning, so the snore must be the work of some holy agent, warning the man to wake, or his wife to wake him, or parson to preach less dully.

Rotello

Taught hens how to lay their eggs in secret places.

Abstrigonius

Lord of ink-blots. He would wait until a scribe had almost completed a beautifully written page of some holy book, and then he would seize the point of the quill and cause it to squirt ink across the page, spoiling the work. His existence could be proved by the fact that monks employed in copying out amusing but unholy books made far fewer blots.

Dozuz

Usually took the form of a jovial
stranger sitting on an inn bench.
He could so bewitch the ale that
an honest fellow who had drunk
but two quarts or three would go
home reeling and bellowing as though
he had drunk twenty.

Dolmira

Consisted of nothing but a smell of aniseed, and caused the
hounds of huntsmen to follow false trails, often leading the
whole hunt into a deep bog.

Pamnesia

Filled the minds of children with idle thoughts, and caused
them to forget their lessons.

Gormiel

Was a small, squat devil, but peculiarly heavy. His task was
to sit invisible on new-kneaded dough and prevent it from
rising.

(*Note :* It is strange that no authority mentions a fiend who
sits on the shoulders of other authorities, whispering to them
lists of imaginary fiends, and thus wasting their own time and
their readers'.)

A CHEYENNE SORCERER

So far I've mainly written about the familiar English (and American) sorts of witch. Even in Europe there were many other kinds—the Finnish weather witches, who carried a piece of string curiously knotted in which they could loose or bind the winds—the terrifying cannibal witches of the German forests—and further east still the strange monsters of the Russian imagination, such as Baba Yaga with her house which raced about on two huge chicken-legs.

And outside Europe there were, and still in places are, types of witch who by quite different means acquired magical powers which their peoples believed to be completely real. Very often these witches had to go through appalling rituals, complete changes of behaviour and personality, in order to acquire their powers.

For instance among the Cheyenne there were warriors called Hohnuhke, which means Contraries. In order to retain his magic a Contrary had to do everything by opposites. If he called to a man "Go!" it meant that he wanted him to come nearer, or if he told his woman he wanted food it meant that he was not hungry. He had to live almost alone, and behave with great dignity all the time, though if he sat down he always had to sit on the naked ground. He must never step in another man's footprints, and even in battle he had to charge to one side of main charge.

His magic lived in a decorated weapon, half bow, half lance, which was not used for fighting, but which caused enemy bows to break and enemy guns to misfire. It also prevented the Contrary from being struck by lightning, which was what he was most afraid of, having been warned of the danger in a dream. He had to carry this lance wherever he went, and never let the point touch the ground. If anybody else, even a child or horse, touched the lance, they immediately had to be purified by being rubbed with white sage, otherwise the lightning would kill them.

The lance had two uses, first when pursuing enemies and second when fighting them. If the Contrary unsheathed the point and stuck it into the footprints of enemies whom his tribe were tracking, or if he simply walked on their footprints himself, the enemies' strength of foot would fail, and they would be overtaken. The Contrary could also lame any horses that had been stolen from his tribe by prodding their hoof-prints with the lance.

In battle the Contrary carried the lance in the crook of his left arm, where it must have been a thorough nuisance as he wasn't allowed to use it to fight with, so it could only get in the way of his other weapons. While he was carrying it like this, he was allowed to fight like any other warrior, wheeling, advancing and retreating, according to the nature of the fight. But when, at the climax of the fight, he moved the bow to his right hand, blew on a magic whistle and uttered the cry of a burrowing owl, then he had to charge straight at the enemy until he reached their lines, for that was the magic which caused their bows to break and their guns to misfire.

It was uncomfortable all the time, being a Contrary, and dangerous some of the time. No man willingly became one— the fear of lightning forced him to take the lance. But once having become a Contrary he could not lay the task aside until someone else in his tribe dreamed the warning dream. Then this man would buy the lance from the old Contrary, who could give up his rituals and his powers and become an ordinary warrior again.

Seal of the Anti-slavery Society

VOODOO

It began with coffee, rum, tea and sugar.

Haiti is the western half of the island that used to be called Hispaniola. Once it was the most money-making colony in the world, and it belonged to the French. To work the plantations they imported slaves, fresh-caught from Africa, packing them like sardines into the slow sailing-boats that made the deadly 'middle passage' across the Atlantic. They brought them over in incredible numbers, nearly a million in all. In twelve years before the great slave revolt of 1791 they imported 313,200 slaves into Haiti—men who had grown up free, knowing nothing but a forest clearing or a single mountainside, and were now wrenched from their homes, jumbled together and forced to work in conditions of frightful cruelty on the plantations. At the plantation of Sucrerie Cottineau, for instance, the slaves died so fast that the complete working force had been replaced in nine years.

The revolt, when it came, was very bloodthirsty and lasted fourteen years. It shook the world, for it was the only example of a black colony making itself free, and free for black men. The white nations could not afford to acknowledge that it existed at all—it took the United States nearly sixty years to do so, for instance—so for many years Haiti was almost completely isolated. And its original citizens were men who had never had time to learn the religion of their masters, or to forget the strange gods they had worshipped in Africa. So when Europeans started to take an interest in Haiti once more they found, among other things, that it now had a religion of its own, an extraordinary mish-mash of many beliefs, including Christianity. All the experts agree that the proper word for it is not Voodoo, but none of them agree what it is: Vaudou? Vodun? Let's call it Voodoo.

"This is one of the vilest, cruelest and most debased forms of worship ever devised by man," says Dennis Wheatley. "Voodoo is in fact simply a folk religion. Voodoo worshippers are indignant if it is suggested they are not Catholics," says Lucy Mair, who makes it sound quite cosy.

In fact it is just the sort of religion that you would expect an extremely poor and isolated, but naturally happy people to cobble together. It is full of music and excitement and dancing and hysterical ecstasy which is a relief from the harsh world. But it also has its dark side. Practically everybody on the island believes to some extent in witchcraft, and many—even if they are not themselves witches—take magical precautions.

All of us have heard, from films, TV and comics, about *zombies*. What is supposed to happen is this: a strong witch, called a *boko*, will steal a man's soul from him by magic, so that the man appears to die. When his family have buried him, the *boko* will dig him up and revive him by passing under his nose the bottle containing the victim's soul. The man will then rise from his grave and follow his master, moving with leaden limbs, to do whatever he is commanded, to till his fields or murder his enemies. He cannot be killed, and though slow he is tireless. He needs no wages and only the cheapest food, so the witch will prosper. The zombie's only release comes if his master allows him to eat salt. At la Hasco, it is said, there was a *boko* called Joseph who kept three zombies to cut sugar-cane. One day his wife gave them food which happened to contain a few salted peanuts. The sharp

Voodoo dance : the man is possessed by the spirit of one of the gods

salt cleared their minds and they understood what had been done to them. They hurled themselves on their master, tore him apart and wrecked his house; then, staring straight in front of them they raced with extraordinary speed back to their native valley. Some of their own friends and family saw them pass, and called in vain but did not dare to bar their way, knowing how dangerous it is to meddle with the dead. When they reached their own graves they knelt, and with their bare hands began to dig . . .

(This sort of thing is a common African belief. The Bakweri, who live on the slopes of a volcano in West Cameroon, say that among them are *nyongo*, who have the power to take dead people away to work for them without wages on another mountain, sixty miles to the north, where the nyongo-men, thanks to this free labour, have everything they need, including electricity in their huts and new Fords standing outside. If you bury a dead *nyongo* he will rise, but if you bury him face down he will be tricked into working his way deeper and deeper into the ground.)

The more sceptical Haitians may also believe in zombies, but they say that the *boko* uses a mind-destroying poison, which makes the victim seem dead. When he is dug up again the *boko* gives him an antidote which enables him to move but not to think or remember. There's no evidence that this is true, either. Those who believe it only substitute a rational nightmare for a fantastic one.

But zombies are not the only form of witchcraft that haunt the island. If you wish to kill an enemy, you cause his image to appear reflected in a bucket of water. Stab the water and if it reddens with blood the man will die. Or go to a stone that belongs to Baron-Samedi, Lord of the dead; strike your hand-axe three times against the stone, saying "Baron-Samedi" as you do so. If Baron-Samedi is willing his spirit will fill you. Then you take a sacrifice of chopped fruit to a cemetery, offer it to one of the crosses and take earth from the grave. Spread this earth across a path where your enemy will walk, and for each handful you spread the soul of a dead man will enter your enemy and eat his own soul away.

Or you can become a were-wolf (which needn't actually be a wolf). A man was walking at night along a path when he met a cow who would not let him pass, and whom after a while he realised must be a malignant spirit. Luckily this man had recently been to a Voodoo ceremony where his stick had been blessed, so he took courage and begun to beat the cow as hard as he could. All of a sudden he found he was beating the local police-chief. Naturally, he apologised for the mistake, but the police-chief was equally apologetic and begged the man not to tell anyone about the incident. Next day he learnt that the police chief was too ill to get up, and in a few days he was dead, his body all covered with great red weals, as though someone had beaten him with a stick.

Or there are the secret societies of sorcerers who swoop about by night in a great motor-car with violet headlamps, stealing men, turning them into animals and selling them in the market for meat. How else should a cow have a gold tooth? Or vampires . . .

The list is endless. As everywhere, ill chance makes witches, so that there is someone to blame. And, as everywhere, there has to be some protection against witches, and in Haiti it is Voodoo.

Voodoo is a religion of drums and dancing. During the ceremonies the gods descend and enter into the bodies of the worshippers, so that a mild and gentle woman will suddenly begin to swagger and strut, and smoke a big cigar, and swear like a soldier, because she is possessed by Ogu-badagri, the ferocious general who sends the thunder. Or a man will climb up into the ceiling and coil himself down from a beam, hissing his words because he is now Damballah-wedo, the serpent god. Even appalling Baron-Samedi is a popular visitor, wearing a tall hat and several pairs of spectacles and making coarse jokes at which everyone laughs.

This is excitement, this is dream made real, this is the songs of the gods and the thudding drums. This is good luck, and power and protection from witches—protection so strong that it allows a man to beat a malignant cow into an apologetic police-chief.

The late 'Papa Doc' Duvalier was dictator of Haiti. He controlled the island with ferocious gangs of private police called the Tonton Macoutes. His government was both cruel and corrupt. Part of his power came from a widely held belief, which he encouraged, that he was also Baron-Samedi, Lord of the Dead. To be ruled by a man who can destroy your body for a whim is bad enough, but it's nothing to the dread of a monstrous god who can enslave your soul.

Does this make Voodoo wicked? Or would Papa Doc have used any religion for his own purposes, as some dictators have successfully used Christianity? Voodoo was no doubt easier to use, but Papa Doc didn't depend on that. He depended on ignorance, poverty and fervour of belief. I myself would guess that without Voodoo and its excitements the Haitians would have endured an even more miserable time under his reign.

'Papa Doc' Duvalier

If witchcraft worked, what would witches be like in the society we have today?

MR MONNOW

As Mike passed the call-box the phone in it rang.

He was surprised, because he didn't know that the phones in call-boxes could ring like that, and besides this box had an 'Out of Order' card in it. Curious, he stepped into the box and picked the receiver up.

"Hello," he said.

"Mike," said a soft voice.

"Yes, but . . ."

The voice began to chant a string of strange long words. They didn't mean anything to Mike, though he thought they sounded scientific. At first he waited for a pause in which to interrupt, but then he simply listened. The receiver seemed to become very cold, and the cold began to flow into his skull and through his whole body, tingling as it made its way along the individual veins. The chant stopped.

"You will come to me now, Mike," said the voice. "Take the north lift to floor twenty-one and ring the bell of apartment eight."

"All right," said Mike, and found that he was able to put the receiver down at last.

The chill and tingling continued while he walked on down the wide street that led from school to the towering apartment block in which he lived. His friend Paula called to him from the swings near the north entrance, but he didn't notice. His body twitched from sheer habit at the sixth floor, where he usually left the lift, but he stayed where he was while the lift rose and rose.

On his own floor there were only seven apartments, but on the twenty-first he found a door marked '8' where he would have expected to find the cupboard that contained the heating duct controls. When he pressed the bell the door opened at

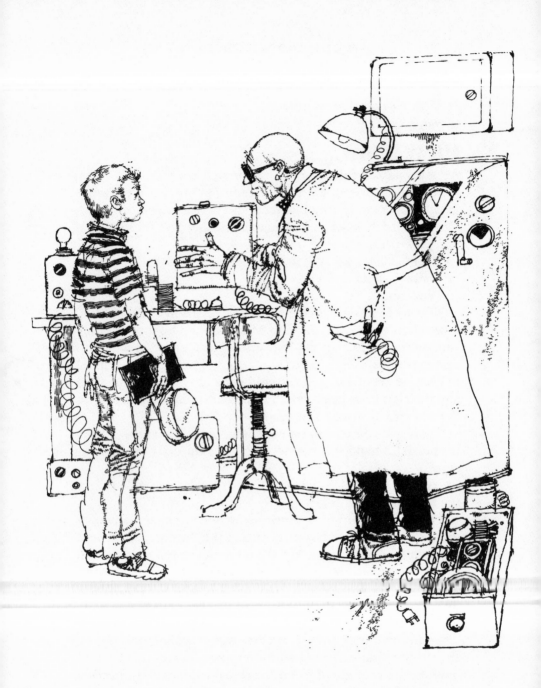

once. As he went in the cold, compelling spirit left him and he became just ordinary Mike again.

The first thing he saw was that he was not in a living-room but a workshop, with blinds drawn down the windows and soft yellow lamps lighting benches covered with equipment, some of it boxed and tidy but other bits made only of trailing wires and knobby objects and dials. All of it hummed and winked, fizzed and sparked.

A man in grey overalls was working at the far bench, but he swung round as the door closed.

"Hello, Mike," he said. "Nice of you to come. I'm Mr Monnow."

It was the same soft voice. He was rather small and his skin was pale and strange. In fact Mike felt he could see a little way into it; it reminded him of the pallid plants they had grown in the dark for a biology experiment. Mr Monnow wore very black sunglasses.

"Well, er . . ." said Mike.

"Shan't keep you long," said Mr Monnow. "How's things at school?"

"OK," said Mike, "except I've got returned work for maths. I usually do."

"Well, that's no problem," said Mr Monnow, almost like a doctor who has been asked to cure some very simple ailment. "Come and stand over here, Mike. This will only take a few seconds."

Mike started to try and think of some excuse, but then he found that his legs had obeyed the order, and that his tongue refused to protest as Mr Monnow lifted a box from one of the benches, adjusted two or three controls, and lowered it over Mike's head. The strange thing was that there seemed to be no mechanism at all inside the box, only a furry dark that clicked rapidly. His brain went floating away, weaving around the clicks. Then he was standing in the workshop again, blinking at the dim lights.

"Feel all right?" said Mr Monnow. "Good. Got a text-book with you? Good. Why not see what you make of the stuff that's been bothering you?"

Mike turned the hated, baffling pages and started to read. He found himself turning the page and reading on, without having to go back at all. He skipped the exercises, because they were all so obvious once he'd read the explanations and examples. It was the same with pages further on, which he hadn't even begun yet, and when he turned back he couldn't remember what he'd found so difficult only that morning.

"That's great!" he whispered. "Oh, thank you!"

"Glad to be of help," said Mr Monnow. "Now, there's something I'd like you to do in exchange. I need to, er, interview a few people, and I can't go out and find them because I've got a skin-disease which makes me sensitive to ultra-violet rays. Even ordinary daylight, with no sunshine, would kill me in a very short time. So what I want . . ."

"Mike," said Paula. "What's the matter, Mike?"

"Nothing."

"You've got to tell me."

"I can't."

This was true. Mr Monnow had simply told Mike not to tell anyone, and so he couldn't. It was impossible. He couldn't even explain to his maths teacher why he was suddenly doing so well.

Paula looked at him, sighed and gazed up at the soaring dark perspective of the tower. Far up, tiny with distance, her big brother Rob dangled in his cradle washing a line of windows. Paula's Dad was the engineer in charge of all the heating and lighting in the Tower, which was why Paula knew everything about everybody.

She put out her cold little hand and touched his wrist.

"Mike," she said.

"I can't . . ." he began. But he found he could. It was

marvellous to tell somebody.

"But that's horrible," she said when he'd finished. "Is that what happened to Mrs Berwick?"

Old Mrs Berwick had been found wandering up and down the stairways, unable to remember the number of her own floor and apartment. She was in hospital now.

"She was a bit gaga anyway," said Paula, trying to make it sound less awful.

"Not really, she wasn't," said Mike. "I told him I wanted to stop and he said he was terribly sorry, but . . . and then he pressed this switch. It isn't . . . I mean it doesn't . . ."

There were no words for the instant of unbeing which Mike had known before the switch clicked back. But Paula nodded.

"What does he want them for?" she said.

"He told me—he doesn't mind what he tells me—he thinks I belong to him. He's building a new sort of computer. You know in an ordinary computer there are a lot of little cells—all they can do is be switched on or off—that means say yes or no to a question—but if you put a lot of them together they can answer very complicated questions? Well, he's not using cells—he's using people's brain-circuits."

"Any people? Old people? I mean, Mrs Berwick was a *bit* gaga, even before?"

"No, he was just experimenting with them, because he thought no one would mind if they went . . . like Mrs Berwick. But now he wants me to start bringing some of my friends."

"Me?"

"No, Tom Turner. Tom's been away sick this week, which has held him up, but . . . Paula, I don't know what to do!"

Paula scuffled her heel through the scraped earth under her swing. Mike stared dully up at the clean rectangle of the tower, tier on tier of people-cells. He saw that it was rather like the picture of a computer storage unit in one of his schoolbooks . . . perhaps in the end Mr Monnow would turn it into just that.

"But will it do Tom any harm?" said Paula. "I mean, *you're* just the same, except for the maths."

"He added with me," said Mike. "With Tom he's going to subtract."

"How do you do that with the door, Mr Monnow?" asked Mike. "I came to look one day when you hadn't sent for me, and it was just a locked cupboard, like on the other floors."

"It is a mathematical manipulation of space," said Mr Monnow. He had made only one small gesture of impatience on hearing that Tom was still poorly, but had been calm and polite, as always.

"Then aren't we here at all?"

"Your question is meaningless. But if you mean does the manipulation apply to the whole room, the answer is no. I would like it, but I cannot afford the drive. You can prove for yourself that we are still in the tower, because I would like you to operate my scanner and see if you can find somebody to replace Tom. I do not care to stand close to the window on so bright a day."

Mike would have liked to ask more about 'drive'. Mr Monnow had mentioned it once or twice, explaining why all the equipment, which looked so electrical, was not connected to any power supply. Its energy came from 'drive'. But now Mike had to concentrate on the instructions for working the scanner. This had a dish aerial like a radar scanner, but also an eyepiece like a telescope. Mike's job was to pick out someone in the street below, focus on them by turning two knobs, and then check three dials. If all three needles lay on the narrow blue segment of their dials, that person was suitable.

As soon as he was sure Mike had understood, Mr Monnow went well away from the window and told Mike to release the blind. It fizzed up, and there, dizzily below, lay the wide street leading to school. There, tiny, was the call-box. This was how Mike himself had been 'found'.

He didn't find anyone himself, that morning. In a way this was a relief. On the other hand when Mr Monnow thanked him and said goodbye, there was something slightly different about his tone.

"I don't know what to do!" said Mike.

"I expect Tom will go on being sick for a bit," said Paula, as though she was in fact sure of it. She was still the only person Mike was able to talk to about the horrible trap he had landed in, but she wasn't much use. Mike shook his head.

"He's getting impatient," he said. "If we don't find somebody else soon, he's going to use *me*! He hasn't said so, but I know."

"That's bad," said Paula. "You must get him to let you use that scanner thing whenever you go."

"But what'll I do if I do find somebody?" whispered Mike. "I mean, why should they . . ."

"It's you or them, Mike."

"Yes, but . . ."

Paula smiled and began to swing, gazing as she did so up at the glass cliff of the tower. She wasn't any use at all.

"Hello, Mike," said Mr Monnow as usual. "Good of you to come. Now I want you to help me with a little experiment."

Mike had become so sensitive to the almost toneless soft voice that he could hear the faint prickle of excitement behind the words. His heart seemed to double its size in an instant, pounding uselessly away, while his palms and cheeks were icy with sudden sweat.

"Couldn't I try the scanner once more?" he whispered. "There's still a lot of kids coming back from school."

Mr Monnow hesitated.

"If you wish, for a few minutes, while I arrange my instruments," he said.

Mike opened the blind and set the scanner. Groups of kids were still loitering back towards the tower. He picked a group that was just passing the call-box, aimed the optical scanner at them and peered through the eyepiece. Misty coloured shapes swam about at the bottom of a dim grey well, but as he turned the knobs the shapes became hard-edged, and then he was looking as if from a few feet away at a black girl called Laurie something. He hardly knew her at all. She was laughing. Once focussed, the scanner locked itself automatically onto her, so that she stayed in the middle of the picture even when she danced sideways to make a mock attack on one of her friends. Mike raised his head from the eyepiece and looked at the dials. All three needles quivered in the middle of their blue segment. Laurie would do.

His mouth opened, but he couldn't say the words.

"I'm ready now," said Mr Monnow.

Mike gave one of the focus knobs a quick twist and saw the needles dart away from the blue segments.

"Please," he whispered, turning into the room, "can't you . . ."

But Mr Monnow's hand was poised above the switch that had once sent through all Mike's nerve-fibres that flood of icy nothing. Mike swallowed, and waited for what had happened to Mrs Berwick to begin to happen to him. The light from the window behind him darkened. Mr Monnow frowned, then made a dash for the blind. Mike moved too slowly to attempt to trip him, but suddenly the room was full of blinding light, mauve and as strong as lightning, searing through Mike's shut eyelids. It lasted only as long as a photo flash, but in that instant Mr Monnow screamed and Mike heard him fall.

He opened his eyes and saw Mr Monnow lying on the floor and the window-cleaning cradle sliding away out of sight behind the glass. Paula's brother Rob was standing on it, holding something that looked like an enormous silver reflector-lamp. He waved cheerily to Mike as he passed out of sight, as though he were standing on firm ground and not dangling two hundred feet above it.

Mike's eyes began to hurt, but through his tears he saw that the room had changed. The equipment had changed. The jumble of casings and valves and magnetic coils and dials was now a jumble of cardboard boxes and old bottles and rough circles of paper and a few mattress springs. But Mr Monnow still lay on the carpet. His sunglasses had come off as he fell, and now Mike could see that he had no eyes at all, no eye-sockets, only smooth pale flesh running up from his cheek-bones to his forehead.

"I expect he was light-sensitive all over, so he didn't need eyes," said Paula, matter-of-fact as ever. Mike's own eyes still hurt, so he kept them half closed, which made Paula look old, very old, a little old woman hundreds of years old.

"I suppose I ought to thank Rob," he said.

"Don't bother," said Paula. "He thought it was a lark."

"There's one thing I don't understand—I mean there's a lot of things I don't understand."

"That's right," said Paula.

"But there *is* one thing," Mike insisted. "That ultra-violet lamp Rob got hold of—I saw it quite clearly before my eyes began to hurt, and I saw there wasn't any cable for the power supply. It must have taken a lot of power. It ran off 'drive', didn't it?"

Paula rocked her swing a few inches and sighed. Then she laid her hand, always strangely cold, on Mike's wrist. The cold began to flow into his arm and through his whole body, tingling as it made its way along the individual veins.

"You'd better forget about that, Mike," she said. "You'd better forget about the whole thing."

The tingling cold seemed to flow back into her hand. By the time it was all gone Mike had forgotten.

DESTINY

a dream you cannot quite remember
the shadow of the huntsman
a falling tree
the gleam on the sea as the journey ends
a room you are never allowed into
a lake in a pine forest

KING OEDIPUS

Thebes was a strong city, white-walled and rich. Its king was named Laius, a quick-tempered man who had had the bad fortune to offend some God even quicker-tempered than he. So when he sent (as kings did in those days) to the great oracle at Delphi, the navel of the world, to ask what luck lay in store for his new-born son, the messengers came back with the hideous prophecy that the boy would grow to a man who would kill his own father and marry his own mother.

This was not one of the God's riddling answers which could be interpreted in many ways. The messengers were terrified, but they swore that they had heard through the

lips of the priestess the voice of the God, speaking a single sentence, clear as well-water. When they speak like that, the gods do not lie.

So, weeping, Laius took the infant prince and left him on the bare mountainside where the wild beasts roamed. This

was common practice in those days, with unwanted babies; the child would die, but the parents would (they thought) be guiltless of the actual sin of murder. And Laius, to make extra sure, drove a spike through the baby's heels, pinning him to the ground, and left, still weeping, with his hands over his ears to close out the long wail that troubled the mountain air.

But a shepherd on the mountain heard that wail and found the baby and saw not only that he was beautiful but that he was richly clothed. So he picked him up, bandaged the wounded heels, and carried him to his home across the mountain. Then, feeling that it was wrong that a child of noble birth should be reared in a peasant's hut, he took him down to Corinth and showed him to the King who ruled in that city.

This King and his Queen were childless. Struck with the baby's beauty, they paid the shepherd and took Oedipus and brought him up as their son in Corinth, never telling him the truth. The name they gave him meant swell-foot, but in fact his wound healed and he grew handsome and strong, though quick-tempered like his true father.

Then, when he was a grown man, he went to Delphi himself to learn what fortunes and what perils the fates had set about his future path. And the priestess, rocking in her trance over the crack in the earth from which the strange vapours rose that allowed her to lose her own soul and speak with the mouth of the God, answered with a single sentence, clear as well-water. Oedipus would murder his father and marry his mother.

Oedipus left Delphi, walking along the white road in the cold trance of shock.

Meanwhile at Thebes a nightmare season had come. A monster had flown from the south and perched on the cliffs by the road to the city, a thing with the face of a beautiful woman, body of a lion and wings of an eagle. It was the Sphinx, and it was almost as old as the world.

It perched by the road and asked the passers-by a riddle that was also almost as old as the world, and when they failed to answer (as all did) it dashed them down to the rocks below. As a result few travellers or merchants cared to pass along the road to Thebes, and trade became bad.

King Laius, knowing the duties of a monarch, determined to go to Delphi to ask the God what should be done, and if He, perhaps, knew the answer to the fatal riddle. He took his chariot out by a back way over the hills and rejoined the road beyond where the Sphinx laired. The charioteer lashed the horses, the dust-cloud rose behind the wheels and hung there in a long plume, and so they came to a cross-roads.

Cross-roads have always been places of destiny. It is there that a man must choose which path he will take, and so perhaps choose his whole future life. At this particular cross-roads fate waited for two men, a father and a son.

For it was there that Oedipus stood. He had pulled himself out of his shock enough to know that there was one road that he could not take, the road back to Corinth, where he believed his father waited for the sword and his mother for the dreadful marriage. But all King Laius's charioteer saw was a young traveller blocking the road.

He shouted, but the traveller did not move.

The king was in a hurry.

"Drive the fool down," he snarled.

The charioteer shouted again and the long whip cracked over the foam-flecked manes. Oedipus, in his daze of grief and indecision, was suddenly aware of the racing hooves almost on him. He leapt to one side and as the chariot banged past struck out in sudden rage at the passenger. His staff was tough and well-weighted. The king's neck snapped like the wishbone of a chicken.

So, after twenty years of patient lurking, fate had leapt from its lair and in one moment, at the movement of a dozen muscles, half the prophecy came true.

The charioteer jumped down to avenge his master, but
seeing how tall and fierce the traveller looked he thought
better of it. He put the king's body into the chariot and took
it on to Corinth, whence he sent home a message that Thebes
would have to look for a new lord.

But Oedipus took the road to Thebes, a prince without a
kingdom. He may have thought he was seeking his fortune,
but he was seeking his fate.

He came to a place where the road wound up into the hills
and reached a saddle from which he could look down into a
rich plain, ruled by a richer city. As he stood, leaning on his
staff and looking at the view, a voice crooned at him from
beside the road. He turned and was caught.

He did not see the gold plumes of her wings, the hooked
claws of her pads, the smooth human skin of her neck. Her
dark and ageless gaze filled all his vision. He drowned in that
hypnotic stare.

"Play my game, traveller," sang the Sphinx.

Oedipus had no tongue to answer. The Sphinx sang on.

> *Four-legged at dawn,*
> *Two-legged by day,*
> *Three-legged at eve,*
> *What creature, say?*

The stories do not tell us how Oedipus found the answer.
Perhaps the God put it into his mind, to force him towards
his fate. Perhaps his foster-mother had told him. Perhaps
he had spent the day thinking about youth and age, and the
weakness of small children, and his own strength, and the
weakness that would come again when his neck too could be
broken by a sudden blow from a stranger's staff.

"It is Man," he muttered.

With a tearing wail the Sphinx spread its wings, rose,
circled three times while it found height, and flew south,
still wailing. The sound of its cry brought the citizens of
Thebes to the walls and they saw it go, so they came out to

welcome the stranger who had driven the monster away. And there were feasts and games in Thebes, until the news came from Corinth that their king was dead, killed in a way-side scuffle. They sent and brought his body home and buried it with pomp, and then, since he had been childless, they chose as their new king the young hero who had rescued the city. To confirm him in his office they made him marry the old King's wife, Jocasta, dark and quiet, but troubled with a vague fear that seemed to have persisted out of an otherwise forgotten dream. To each of them this marriage to a total stranger must have seemed a release from all such fears, a proof that the God had lied.

Few exiled princes, Oedipus thought, can have found their fortune so fast. So he ruled Thebes for a while in peace.

But then a new trouble struck Thebes, worse than the Sphinx. A sickness began to creep from house to house, which made all whom it infected lie raving for a night and a day and then rush out into the street, stagger around, cry and fall dead. The Greeks had good doctors, but they knew no cure.

Again the king's duty was clear, though he was a new king. He sent to Delphi, to ask the God the cause of the plague. (Apollo, the God of prophecy, was also the God of sickness and healing, and his sister Artemis was Goddess of cross-roads.) The messenger brought back the God's word, that a single man had brought deadly pollution to Thebes. Oedipus raged, and swore that with his own hand he would punish that man.

Jocasta, troubled again with mysterious fears, warned him not to search too hard. The blind prophet Tiresias warned him also. They only made him more obstinate to riddle the matter clear, as he had with the Sphinx. Tiresias with his inward eye had seen dark glimpses of the truth, and in the end Oedipus forced him to speak, and so the new king learnt that the old king's death was somehow part of the cause of the God's anger. Oedipus himself, between the first shock of hearing the oracle and the second shock of meeting the Sphinx had almost forgotten that scuffle at the cross-roads, but he sent fresh messengers to search for the charioteer, so that it might be known how Laius had died.

And now the news came that the King and Queen of Corinth were dead also. The man who brought the news was an old shepherd who had served them many years, looking after their flocks on the mountainside. Grieving, but eager to prove to Tiresias and the people how the God had lied, Oedipus told the tale of the oracle, and called on the shepherd to witness that the prophecy had not come true.

"No, Lord," said the shepherd in a troubled voice. "My master and mistress were never your parents. It was I that found you on the mountainside and carried you to their court, all bloody with the wounds where a spike had been driven through your heels."

Somewhere, a little to one side, Jocasta opened her mouth to scream, but no sound came. Oedipus did not notice as she moved blindly towards her own rooms, for at that moment there was a cry at the doors and a frightened man was dragged into the court. His guards released him and moved back. He stood, staring round at old friends, but suddenly his eyes fixed on the one new face. His arm shot up.

"That is the man who killed my master!" he cried.

He was pointing straight at Oedipus.

And then the older courtiers began to remember how long ago a baby prince had been born, and because of some prophecy had been carried away to die on the mountainside with a spike through his heels.

The scars of those old wounds began to ache. A scream rose from the Queen's rooms. Stone-faced, Oedipus rushed towards the sound. Among the shrieking women he found Jocasta, his wife, his mother, hanged from a beam, dead by her own hand.

That was his last sight of this world, for with a violent spasm he tore his own eyeballs from their sockets.

That very evening he left Thebes, a blind old wanderer, to beg his way along the roads of Greece.

And at Delphi, for no reason the priests could interpret, the trance-held priestess laughed with the voice of the God.

THE MISTY PATHS OF FATE

Until a thing happens, it is only one of a number of things that might happen. It is a chance among a lot of other chances. As it comes nearer the chances lessen.

A horsewoman is cantering across a field. Both she and the horse have plenty of choices before them, but she decides to jump a particular gap in the hedge, twitches the reins slightly and heads for that place. The choices lessen, though still a

dog might bark and make the horse shy away, or the woman might see the wire early enough to pull up.

But she doesn't. They are already committed to the leap when she sees the dark, dangerous line above the twigs. Now there are very few choices and not many more chances. If she is good enough she may, at that last instant, force her mount to jump higher than his eye tells him he needs to. That's choice. The wire may be rusted enough to snap. That's chance. But there is an instant when she knows they

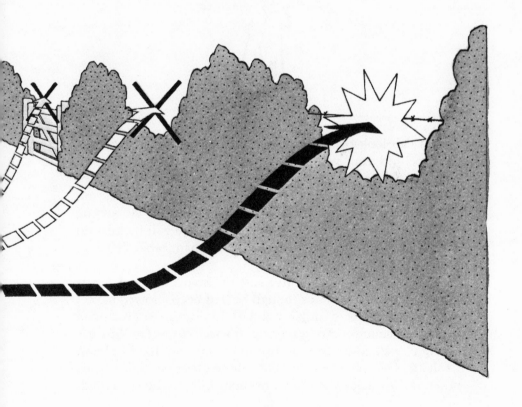

are going to hit the wire, and fall, without choice or chance; and then the green meadow is heeling above her head.

Slowly she picks herself up. Her shoulder hurts, but nothing seems broken. Anxiously she watches the horse struggle to its feet with blood running from a slashed pastern. It can stand, though, and does so patiently while she looks at the gash and feels the bone.

"Lord, we've been lucky!" she whispers.

But all that is fixed. The leap, the reeling world, the fall— nothing can now change any of that. It has happened and become part of her destiny.

You can look back down your life and see it as a zig-zag track behind you, with all your chances fixed into fact and all your choices made. Then you can look ahead and see hundreds of possible tracks branching mistily before you. But you have only to walk a few paces forward and all but one of the nearer tracks will vanish, and that one will be mist no more, but hard fact, gravelled with unchangeable instants. It will have become your destiny.

Oedipus knew his destiny, and his struggles to avoid it made it come true. It's as though he had been allowed to see, clear in the mists, a single point in his future landscape, a solid tree among the wavering tracks. He spent his life trying to walk away from it, but in the end he stood beneath its shade. One can even speculate about other possible tracks, other stories that might have brought him to the same end.

1 Laius disbelieves the God, or the messengers. The prince grows up at Thebes, falls in love with his mother and in order to be able to marry her murders his father.

2 Oedipus, hearing the oracle, decides to kill himself but doesn't want to commit suicide. So he goes back to Corinth and persuades the king to declare war on Thebes so that he can die in battle. But he doesn't. He kills the king of Thebes in the battle and takes the queen as part of his war booty.

3 The God was speaking in riddles after all. Oedipus stays at Thebes, and when he learns of the oracle he does kill himself. So his only bride is the earth he is buried in, and the earth is the mother of us all. Laius dies of grief, and thus Oedipus can be said to have killed him.

And so on.

But most of us, thank heavens, have seen no such tree. Our destinies may go anywhere. Another old story, Little Red Riding-Hood, could have happened a dozen other ways. Over the page there is a chart of some of the other things that might have happened to her in the forest that morning. You can follow her destiny—which is the story as we know it— through the chart. But you can also follow a number of other interlocking adventures she might have had.

The important thing about the chart is that the lines between the boxes represent time, so you can only move along them in the direction of the arrows. Most of the boxes represent choices or chances, so that there is more than one exit from them, but once you've chosen one you can't go back and choose the other. Some boxes have more than one entrance, which means they represent something that would have happened anyway.

The chart doesn't cover all the possibilities, but it's quite complicated enough as it is.

WHAT ELSE MIGHT HAVE HAPPENED TO LITTLE RED RIDING HOOD?

R = Red Riding Hood,   W = Wolf,   G = Grandmother,
H = Huntsman,   P = Prince,   T = Toad. (There is more than one W in the forest.)

START HERE Travel along any line in direction of arrows.

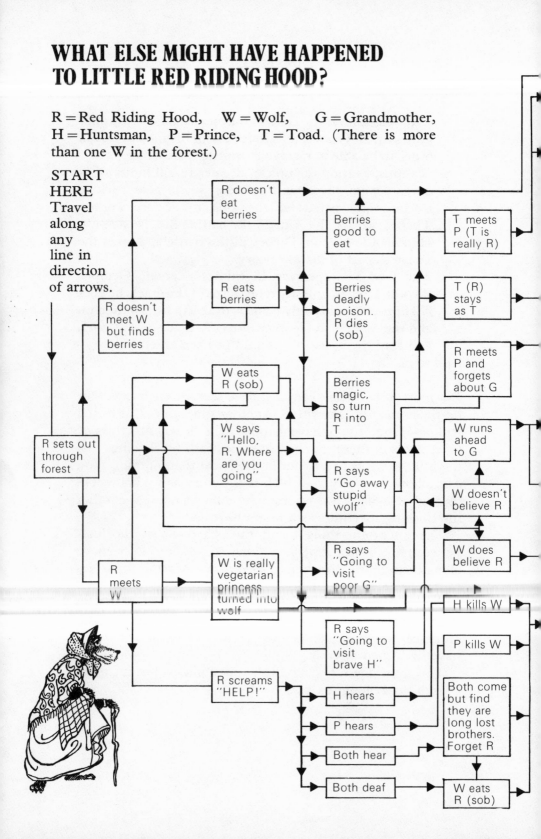

R doesn't eat berries

Berries good to eat

T meets P (T is really R)

R doesn't meet W but finds berries

R eats berries

Berries deadly poison. R dies (sob)

T (R) stays as T

R meets P and forgets about G

W eats R (sob)

Berries magic, so turn R into T

W says "Hello, R. Where are you going"

W runs ahead to G

R says "Go away stupid wolf"

W doesn't believe R

R sets out through forest

W is really vegetarian princess turned into wolf

R says "Going to visit poor G"

W does believe R

R meets W

R says "Going to visit brave H"

H kills W

P kills W

R screams "HELP!"

H hears

P hears

Both come but find they are long lost brothers. Forget R

Both hear

Both deaf

W eats R (sob)

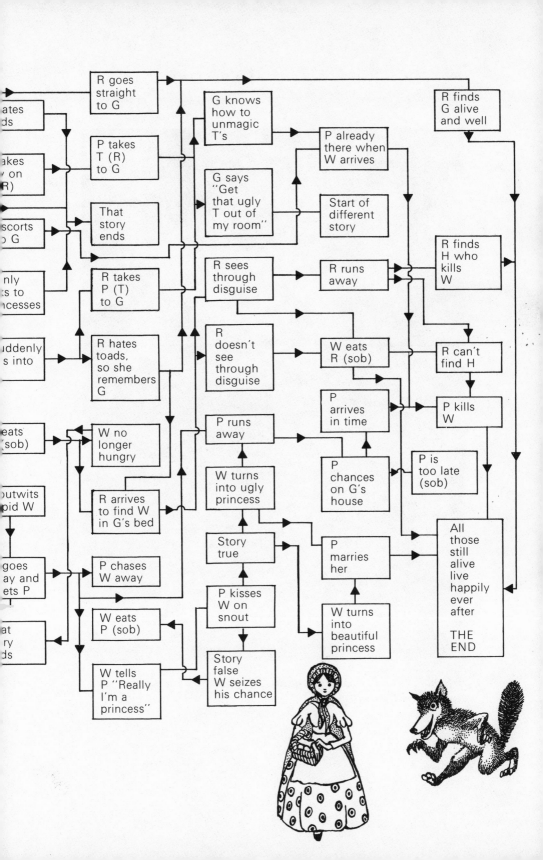

R goes straight to G

...ates ...ds

...akes ...w on ...R)

...scorts ...o G

...nly ...s to ...ncesses

...uddenly ...s into

...eats ...sob)

...utwits ...pid W

...goes ...ay and ...ts P

...at ...ry ...ds

P takes T (R) to G

That story ends

R takes P (T) to G

R hates toads, so she remembers G

W no longer hungry

R arrives to find W in G's bed

P chases W away

W eats P (sob)

W tells P "Really I'm a princess"

G knows how to unmagic T's

G says "Get that ugly T out of my room"

R sees through disguise

R doesn't see through disguise

P runs away

W turns into ugly princess

Story true

P kisses W on snout

Story false W seizes his chance

P already there when W arrives

Start of different story

R runs away

W eats R (sob)

P arrives in time

P chances on G's house

P marries her

W turns into beautiful princess

R finds G alive and well

R finds H who kills W

R can't find H

P kills W

P is too late (sob)

All those still alive live happily ever after

THE END

A female fortune-teller in India. The figure on the ground is the
Goddess of Learning.

IS THE FUTURE FIXED?

In the story, Oedipus was doomed to fulfil his destiny—but it's only a story. His future was fixed, because the plot demands that. We aren't in a story, so we're different. Anything can happen to us, it seems. We are free. But . . .

Take the horsewoman who rides at the gap in the hedge, sees the wire too late and falls. I said that a dog might have barked at the right moment and caused the horse to shy away. But for various reasons there was no dog there, and those reasons already existed. They were facts, as solid as the fall was about to become in a few seconds' time. The woman could have chosen not to jump that gap, but there were reasons why she made her choice—the ride had been dull so far, the horse had refused a gap like that on her last ride, and so on. There were probably a whole pack of reasons, many of which she wasn't aware of, which caused her to make that choice; so for her to choose differently, a different set of reasons would have been needed, but they weren't there. The ones that caused her to make the choice already existed, and nothing could change them. You cannot change the past.

If this argument is right it means that we are prisoners of our own fates, with no command over what we do. The coward was destined to turn and run; nothing could have made him face the guns. The saint was destined to his prayers and exaltations; no temptation could have drawn him from them. Fate put the pistol into the murderer's hand and put this book into yours.

Most of us dislike this argument very much, and instinctively feel that it's wrong. We 'know' we are free to choose—not always, but most of the time. In the past good men have massacred other good men, or burnt them at the stake, because of their different views on fate and free will. (The argument then took a different path: if God knows everything, then he knows what will happen; but if he knows what will happen, then that is fixed and the sinner has been doomed to his wickedness since before the beginning of the world; when God created Adam He knew that he was destined to eat the forbidden fruit; so God in effect decreed the Fall of Man.)

At least nowadays we have a possible escape from the prison of our fate, because modern physics has shown that there is a level of matter at which events seem to happen without causes. It is impossible to know both the position and the momentum of an atomic particle; the more accurately one is fixed, the more of a blur the other becomes. So it is impossible to predict the movement of any particular particle. It also seems to be impossible to cause a particle to behave in a certain way—for instance, although the particles of an unstable element such as Uranium 235 decay at a known rate, it is impossible either to tell when any one particle is going to decay, or to cause it to do so. So here is a space in the great machine of the universe where events seem to have no causes.

Moreover, the events that happen in our brains—memories, decisions, reasonings—also take place somewhere near this level. So it is possible that when I make a choice, that choice is not altogether the result of causes over which I have no control because they themselves are part of an existing chain of causes. Perhaps I can, to some extent, choose my own path.

I hope so, anyway, even if it means that I am also responsible for where that path takes me. I would rather face that than believe that my every sniff and fidget was mapped out for me before I was born.

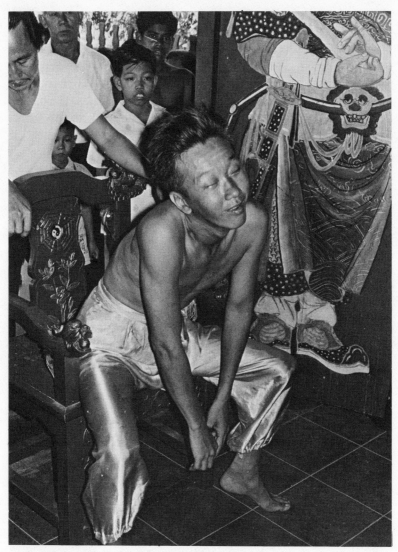

A Chinese medium telling fortunes in a trance

SEEING THE FUTURE

If our destinies are fixed, then perhaps they can be foreseen. Certainly in every time and country there have been men and women who claimed that they could see further into the mists than ordinary men. Some, like the priestess of Delphi, did it by going into a trance, others by gazing into ink-pools or crystal spheres or wells, others by studying the stars or playing-cards or the lines on the palms of our hands. Here are a few of the more exotic methods, which readers may care to try for themselves:

1 Sleep under a waterfall wrapped in raw cow-hide. Then interpret your dreams.

2 Look for signs in the patterns made by the droppings of mice.

3 Listen to the thunder and learn its language.

4 Keep sacred chickens and from time to time kill one and examine its entrails. The spots on the liver (if any) are of especial interest.

5 Keep ordinary chickens, feed them with sacred poison and watch whether and how they die. (This is not strictly a method of telling the future, but is said to be a reliable way of detecting witches, murderers and secret enemies.)

6 Watch for significant shapes in the clouds.

7 Sit in a sacred oak-grove and listen to the language of the leaves as the wind stirs them.

8 Take a sacred book. With your eyes shut, open it at random and place your left little finger on the page. Open your eyes and read the sentence or verse you are pointing at.

But the three great systems of fortune-telling are palmistry, astrology and (in the Western world) card-reading. A full description of any of these would take a book in itself, so all we have room for here is an outline. However, since a lot of readers might like to see whether they themselves have the gift, I've included a full account of one method of telling fortunes with ordinary playing-cards.

General Rules for Fortune-telling with cards

1 Use an old pack of cards, preferably one which you have often handled. If you have a special pack with which you play patience, use that. If you want to go on telling fortunes, keep this pack for that purpose alone. Wrap it up in a piece of cloth, and let no one else handle it.

2 Sit opposite your client—the person whose fortune you are reading—with your back to the north.

3 Whenever you shuffle, do it thoroughly; this is not just to mix the cards, but to build up contact with them.

4 Cut with your left hand only.

5 Turn the cards over end-to-end and not sideways, both when dealing and when turning up cards which have been dealt face down. This means that you will be reading them the same way up as that in which they lay to your client when they were hidden. (In this system this point only matters for the Ace of Spades, but that's an important card.)

6 When the instructions say 'left', it means your left, not your client's.

The 21-card System

I Remove from the pack all the sixes, fives, fours, threes and the two of diamonds, clubs and spades. Put the Two of Hearts to one side for the moment. Later it will be used to represent your client.

2 Shuffle the remaining thirty-two cards.

3 Deal eleven cards face down in a pile to one side, and leave them there till stage 12.

4 Shuffle again, and cut.

5 Lay the top card, face down, by itself. This is called the 'Surprise'.

6 Pick up the Two of Hearts and slide it, at random, into your pack of remaining twenty cards.

7 Shuffle and cut.

8 Deal out the cards face up in an arc in front of you, starting on the left. If you are short of space they may overlap.

9 Place the Surprise card, face down, below the centre of the arc.

10 You can now read the first part of the message from the future. Until you know the meanings of the cards you will need to study the chart and list of combinations on pages 214-218. You should also read the note that follows them on how to interpret the message.

11 When you have got all you can out of the line of cards, you turn the Surprise card over and read that. It is a separate item, but the closer it is to the Two of Hearts in the line above it, the sooner it will happen.

That finishes the general reading of the client's fortune, and perhaps it is all that is needed. If so, proceed at once to stage 18. But if there is some particular matter about which your client wants to consult you, proceed as follows:-

12 Remove the Two of Hearts. Collect the remaining thirty-two cards (including the eleven you laid aside at stage 3), shuffle and cut.

13 Deal eleven cards to one side, as before.

14 Shuffle, cut and deal into three packs, face down.

15 Remove the top card of each pack to form a three-card Surprise and put to one side, face down.

16 Having made sure that you understand the exact point about which your client wants information, ask him/her to choose one of the three packs.

17 Deal the pack he chooses out in a line, face up, with the Surprise face down below. Read them as before (but note there is now no Two of Hearts to relate the cards to so some of the stages are missed out). The line of six cards concerns the immediate answer to your client's problem; the Surprise is more distantly related.

18 The session is now over. Insist on being paid, if only with a kiss. Silver is traditional, and a cube of sugar wrapped in foil will do. But it is an insult to the cards to use them for nothing.

The Meanings of the Cards

	♥	♦	♣	♠
SUIT	Joy, love, the spirit, personal character. The home. Co-operation. Autumn.	Money. Influence. Work. Law suits. Possessions. Greed for gain. Progress. Spring.	Spiritual power. Justice, order, wisdom, security. A warning against idleness, gossip and delay. Summer.	The physical world. The government, the police, soldiers. Obstacles and difficulties, how to conquer them. Winter.
KING	A man. Fair, handsome, mature. Strong character but quick tempered. Generous. Loyal. — HA* DA CA	A man. Perhaps blue-eyed. Strong character but close and ruthless. With women, inclined to jealousy. — HA DQ DJ C8	A man. A true friend, strong and reliable. A good husband or father. — HA	A man, dark and ambitious. Sometimes a soldier. Be careful in all dealings with him. A bad enemy. — S9
QUEEN	A woman, fair and friendly. A loving wife, a pretty woman, a warm nature.	A woman. Pretty but frivolous, selfish and interfering. If with other diamonds, a rich or influential woman, helpful to the client. — DK	A woman, loving and dependable. Inquisitive, but can keep a secret. Generous with money.	A woman. A widow. A strong character. A faithful friend. — SA
JACK	A young man, fair. A friend, but frivolous and gossipy. Not very reliable, though well-meaning.	A businessman. A professional man, paid to help the client. A journey. (For women) A Baby. — SA	A man. A friend. A sign of trouble coming, in which he will help. Honest, and expects honest dealing from others.	A man. Perhaps a doctor or barrister, or a soldier. Disorderly influence, and deceitful. Brave, but selfish. A killer.

TEN	A wealthy visitor. Health after illness. A good marriage. Glamour and publicity.	Good luck. Sudden wealth. A change of life-style. But read the small print. — H8 DA S10	An escape from illness. A large sum of money. If a court-card comes before it, a journey to meet an old friend. — H10 H8 S10	A slight illness. A long journey with a sad end. Secret enemies. Government business. — H7
NINE	The wish card. A wish comes true. Success. Peace.	Water. A sea-journey. Money for a ticket. — H8 C10 S7	Work going better. A business matter out of town.	(A card of power.) Honesty conquers enemies. But also failure. Death of a friend. Legal papers. — C9
EIGHT	If at left, breaking off a mild love affair. At right, fun and company. Flirtation.	A journey involving a new friend, and happiness. Sometimes a difficult childbirth. — C8 S8	Successful business affairs involving friends. But if with diamonds, a warning not to borrow or gamble. — DK D10 CA	Hidden snags. Secret foes. Mistakes caused by haste. A road journey. — S10 S9
SEVEN	A new start, probably after a disappointment. Broken promises. Ultimate success.	Wedding bells. Scandal. Bad luck at gambling. — DQ S7	Good fortune for the honest. If with a court-card of opposite sex to the sitter, a warning against flirtation. — C8	Mistaken quarrels. Loss of a friend. Sorrow. — D10 D9
ACE	Love, passion. Love-letters. With eight of hearts, a proposal. Alone, sometimes an illicit love affair.	A gift. A legacy. An engagement ring. Expensive but successful professional help.	A letter about money (probably earnings, not a windfall). Ambitions achieved. Sudden news at night. — DA D7 SA S10	If right way up: success in love. A tall building. If wrong way up: death, sickness, failure, grief. — HK DJ CQ S7

*If a card shown at the side of some squares lies immediately to the right of the card in question, refer to pages 216-217.

Meanings of touching pairs of cards

(The card first mentioned on pages 214-215 must be on the left.)

King with	Heart Ace	Gambling
	Club Ace	Law courts
	Diamond Ace	Hotel
Eight with	Heart Ace	Marriage
	Diamond Eight	Loss through delay
Seven with	Diamond Seven	Important changes at a distance
	Spade Ten	Loss of some small object

King with	Heart Ace	Dancing
	Diamond Queen	Country people
	Diamond Jack	A business partnership, perhaps father-and-son
	Club eight	A thief
Queen with	Diamond King	A handsome stranger
Jack with	Spade Ace	Waiting for someone
Ten with	Heart Eight	Unexpected journey
	Diamond Ace	A letter to a foreign country
	Spade Ten	Anger
Nine with	Heart Eight	A journey
	Club Ten	A journey overseas
	Spade Seven	Delay
Eight with	Club Eight	A move to the country
	Spade Eight	A quarrel *or* illness
Seven with	Diamond Queen	A fight
	Spade Seven	A good friend

King with	Heart Ace	A bank
Ten with	Heart Ten	An unexpected sum of money
	Heart Eight	An inheritance
	Spade Ten	Money losses
Eight with	Diamond King	Theft
	Diamond Ten	A trip abroad
	Club Ace	A declaration of love
Seven with	Club Eight	Friends bring profit
Ace with	Spade Ace reversed	Prison
	Diamond Ace	A love-letter
	Diamond Seven	A lot of money
	Spade Ten	Jealousy in love

King with	Spade Nine	Poverty
Queen with	Spade Ace reversed	Infidelity in love
Ten with	Heart Seven	A shock
Nine with	Club Nine	False hopes
Eight with	Spade Nine *or* Spade Ten	A road accident
Seven with	Diamond Nine	Separation
	Diamond Ten	Change for the worse
Ace with	Spade Seven	A lawsuit
Ace reversed with	Heart King	Hospital
	Diamond Jack	Someone is waiting for you
	Club Queen	Great injustice

Card Combinations

Special meanings of cards to the right of the Two of Hearts. (The cards need not necessarily be next to each other—it's their general position that matters.) For instance, when you have dealt your cards, you may find the Two of Hearts fifteenth from the left. This means there are four cards to the right of it. You see that three of these are eights. In the panel below, reading across from eights and down from threes, you find 'a bad marriage'.

	4	**3**	**2**
Kings	Dismissal	Consultation	Bad advice
Queens	A crowd of women	Female deceit	Friends call
Jacks	Illness	A petty quarrel	Restlessness
Tens	Legal matters	Social change	Change
Nines	A pleasant surprise	Dull times	A little money
Eights	Financial setback	A bad marriage	A new friend
Sevens	Intrigue	Physical pain	Minor news
Aces	A great surprise	Small successes	Deceit

Special meanings of cards to the left of the Two of Hearts.

	4	**3**	**2**
Kings	Busy times	Trade	Plans
Queens	Bad company	Feasting	Work
Jacks	Sudden need	Idleness	Visitors
Tens	A major event	Poverty	Waiting
Nines	A nasty surprise	Imprudence	Profit
Eights	A bad mistake	A play	Frustration
Sevens	An unjust man	Joy	Harsh words
Aces	Sudden bad luck	Dishonesty	Enemies

HOW TO READ THE CARDS

A good fortune-teller needs both power and skill. The power is needed to draw the message out of the future; the skill is needed to read it. You are like an archaeologist trying to read a battered inscription written in a difficult language. You have to do a lot of guessing and piecing together, and even when you've finished there will be places which don't seem to make much sense.

Try to read the cards together. If a card has several meanings choose the one that seems to fit best with the rest of the message. If two cards contradict each other, ignore the one that fits worse. If a card is part of a touching-pair combination, it is usually best to ignore the meaning it has by itself.

Take your time. It is not cheating to use any knowledge you may have about your client in order to check your message, or to choose between meanings, but it is a mistake to start from what you know and to try to read meanings round that.

When you have dealt your line of cards out, first consider the meanings of the card combinations to left and right of the Two of Hearts, shown on page 218.

Then see whether any particular suits predominate close to the Two of Hearts, and study their meanings as suits (see pages 214-215).

Then, using the rest of pages 214-217, start at the left of the line and try to compose a message. Remember that some cards, particularly those early in the line, may refer to things that have recently happened or are happening now. The cards closest to the Two of Hearts are those with most immediate impact on your client, but a group of cards further away, if their meanings support each other, may have more significance.

Sometimes you seem to get broken bits of different messages; if so, be content with that.

THE TAROT

(The word is pronounced to rhyme with 'arrow'.)

Nobody really knows the origin of these strange cards, though there have been many guesses. In some parts of Europe they are still used as playing cards, mainly for a complicated kind of rummy. Elsewhere they are only used for fortune-telling.

A Tarot pack contains seventy-eight cards, fifty-six of which are divided into four suits of fourteen cards each—Batons, Cups, Swords and Coins. The suits contain the same cards as those in a modern pack, plus an extra colour-card, the Knight, who is shown as a soldier mounted on a horse and comes in order between the Queen and the Jack.

The remaining twenty-two cards are the Greater Trumps, and they show a numbered sequence of symbolic scenes and figures, whose meaning has been explained in many different ways. One theory is that they embody the secret magical wisdom of ancient Egypt. A better idea I think—though there's no way of proving it—is that they were originally made to help teach a secret religion to illiterate people. The religion was Gnosticism (which means the creed of the Knowers). It was partly Christian but the official Christian Church always oppressed and persecuted it. Some of its ideas were used in alchemy and magic. Its main beliefs were that the soul of man, the divine element, had become entangled with dead matter and should be set free; and that the universe was full of spirits and governed by warring powers of good and evil, light and dark.

According to this theory the Greater Trumps are a sort of strip cartoon, showing the soul's path through the world. You can imagine a travelling priest of the Gnostics, a hunted man moving from village to village, sitting in some hovel late one evening. A sentry stands by the door. The priest has laid aside his disguises and sits in the place of honour, wearing flowing robes. There is a star on his forehead. By firelight and lantern light he preaches his secret wisdom, and as he does so the Greater Trumps are passed round through the work-hardened hands of peasants, who peer reverently at the crude pictures and learn their mighty meanings.

Perhaps the priest's disguise was that of a travelling juggler or showman. In that case it would be cunning for him to hide the cards of his forbidden mysteries among other cards which were used for gambling or wayside juggling. It would even be sense to have packs made in which the Greater Trumps appeared to be part and parcel with the rest.

My explanation of the Greater Trumps is only one possible explanation. Sometimes I refer to a detail which may not be in the picture, because no one set of cards follows the main tradition in every instance.

The Fool

He has no number, because he is Man, and the numbered cards are his journey. He sets out carefree, gazing at a gaudy butterfly, while his animal nature in the shape of a dog tears at his leg.

I The Magician

Here is a wayside juggler, all tricks and shows. He is Man in his first discovery of his power over nature, by which the soul is entrapped in the world of things.

II The She-Pope

The first of the Four Earthly Powers. The two female powers are intuitive. The She-Pope is inward-looking and contemplative. She is the soul's power over the body it dwells in.

III The Empress

The second of the Four Earthly Powers. The Empress represents the soul's acceptance of and one-ness with the natural world. She sits amid the abundance of nature.

IV The Emperor

He is the Third of the Four Earthly Powers. The two male powers are of reason. He too is out of doors, and shows Man using his reason to command all nature.

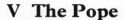

V The Pope

He is the last of the Four Earthly Powers, the power of society, the power Man may have over his fellow men. He is conventional wisdom, which may not be truly wise.

VI The Lovers

This looks simple—a youth between two women, one old, one young. Love hangs aloft, arrow poised. It is the moment of choosing, of inner energies bursting forth, of destiny about to strike.

VII The Chariot

Here the Four Powers are harnessed and united into two strange two-headed horses, which seem as if still trying to tear themselves apart. Man rides forth like a hero to his fate.

VIII Justice

She is a woman, stern-faced, crowned, holding sword and scales. She is conscience, inward doubt at the moment of triumph, the claims of the soul against the world.

IX The Hermit

Here is the Fool again, but how changed! Still journeying, still poor, he has ceased to follow the butterfly, shaken off the dog, and turned his back on worldly triumphs.

X The Wheel of Fortune

This strange symbol shows what happens to the soul that lacks will to continue the journey. Animal he rises, and animal he descends into matter again, and by an animal he is ruled.

XI Fortitude

She stands at the mid point of the journey, wrestling with and overcoming the king of animals, the lion. From now on the journey is that of the spirit.

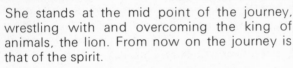

XII The Hanged Man

Is this the Fool again, dangling from the gibbet, calm and young, with his head circled by a halo? The powers of the world cannot harm him, and he sees it all new—upside-down.

XIII Death

The skeleton who reaps crowned heads is a bogy figure, but not to Ones who Know. To them he is only the death of the old worldly self, the door-keeper to the world of the spirit.

XIV Temperance

She is a spirit. She pours the soul, like water, from one vessel to another. She stands with one foot in water and one on land, joining opposites. She is the freedom of the unmixed soul.

XV The Devil

But even in the spirit world are dangers and slaveries, worse than those of the material world. If the Dark Lord cannot be overcome, his service must be endured.

XVI The Tower

The lightning-flash from heaven breaks the prison, casting down and freeing both prisoner and jailer. Here is the moment of illumination, a bolt from the Lord of Light.

XVII The Star

Here is the image of Temperance again, but changed. Now the soul is fully free, poured out not from vessel to vessel but on water and land, an undying stream. A great star signals the mystic moment.

H

XVIII The Moon

Here is a dark path, guarded by wolves, while in the water lurks a primitive crayfish. Even here the spirit, passing through the realms of the Dark Lord, can be trapped back into the prisoning world of matter.

XIX The Sun

And now at last the World of Light where innocence reborn dances in the garden. This is not the innocence of the Fool chasing his butterfly, for it is the Innocence of Knowing.

XX The Judgement

The trumpet is blown at the end of the search. The whole path of past life, right back to childhood, springs up and is renewed and made eternal.

XXI The World

Here is the spirit at the end of its journey, freed from the world and yet at One with it, dancing in a green circle, but watched by angels and animals, who are also the symbols of the four evangelists.

TO CONSULT THE TAROT

There isn't room here to give a complete description of how to read fortunes with a Tarot pack. Anyone really interested had better buy a book—there are several on the subject, including a particularly clear one by Alfred Douglas.

But if you happen to own some Tarot cards and want to give it a try, here is a way of telling somebody's fortune for the next twelve months.

First Remove all the Twos, Threes, Fours, Fives and Sixes.

Second Sit opposite your client. Shuffle the remaining cards. Give them to your client to cut back to you.

Third Deal twelve cards face up in a circle, with a thirteenth card face down in the centre.

Fourth Your circle of cards ought to look like the hour-marks on a clock face. You start at nine o'clock and read the wrong way round the circle, each card being one month of the year. That is to say, the nine o'clock card tells you about next month, the eight o'clock about the month after that, the seven o'clock about the month after that, and so on. The card in the middle sets the general tone for the whole year. You turn it up and read it last of all.

Meanings The most important difference between Tarot cards and ordinary cards is that Tarot cards have a right way up and a wrong way up. If the top of the card is towards the centre of the circle, you interpret it as having a good meaning. If its foot is towards the centre, it has a bad meaning.

For the Greater Trumps, you will have to invent your own meanings (not as difficult as it sounds) on the basis of the picture and the interpretation of it which is given on pages 221-226.

For the minor cards, use the interpretations that I have given for an ordinary pack. Treat the suit of Swords as Spades, Cups as Hearts, Coins as Diamonds and Clubs as Clubs. A Tarot suit contains both a Knight and a Knave. You have to split the meanings of the Jack between these two. The Knight is strong and public, the Knave milder, more subtle and private.

You will find that, in spite of the very brief description I have given, it is in some ways easier to interpret Tarot cards than ordinary cards. Their meanings seem more precise and particular, partly because of the greater interest of the pictures on them, and partly because of their having a right and wrong way up. (In some modern packs, and in some cards of some old packs, the cards are the same both ways up. Confronted with a pack like this, serious fortune-tellers simply write 'Top' and 'Bottom' on each card. That's good enough.)

WHAT THE STARS FORETELL

Certainly, if you gaze up at the stars on a clear night, they have the look of a message. It's hard to believe they don't mean something, if only we could read a pattern into those unnumberable random brightnesses. If only we could crack the code.

Astrologers believe that they can. Although they accept modern astronomy, and have worked new planets into their system as they were discovered, their code is still based on the idea that the earth is a fixed point round which the sun and moon, all the planets, and finally the stars themselves, all move, fixed to revolving transparent spheres. Thus it appears to a man standing on the earth that as the year proceeds the sun slowly works its way across the background of the fixed stars. The man cannot see the stars at the same time that he can see the sun, but by watching what stars are on the eastern horizon just before sunrise he can know where the sun is in relation to them.

(What is really happening is that the earth is taking a year to travel round the sun. As it moves we see the sun from a different angle, with a different set of fixed stars behind it.)

To the man who gazes night by night, year by year, at the sky, the sun also appears to move a little north and south in its path through the heavens, so that it covers a narrow belt of stars. This belt is called the Zodiac, and by tradition it is divided into twelve equal sections, called Houses, whose names are Aries, Taurus, Gemini, Cancer, Leo, Virgo, Libra, Scorpio, Sagittarius, Capricorn, Aquarius and Pisces.

The planets also appear to move, in paths more complicated than the sun's, through the Houses of the Zodiac. The moon counts as a planet.

A serious astrologer, in order to cast your horoscope, will need to know the date, time and place of your birth. From

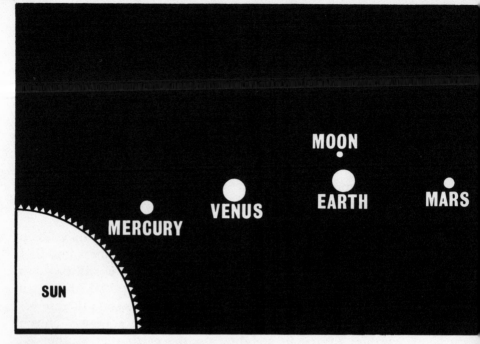

Sun *Generous, warm, arrogant, lazy*
Mercury *Quick, witty, shallow, dishonest*
Venus *Gentle, cheerful, clownish, wanton*
Moon *Artistic, calm, timid, cheerful*
Mars *Brave, forthright, bullying, cruel*

the date he will be able to calculate which Houses the sun and the planets were then in, and from the time and place he will be able to do the rather trickier job of calculating exactly which House was heaving up over the horizon when you drew your first breath. This House is known as the Ascendant, and is the most important single factor in your fate and character, but may well be modified by other factors.

For instance, Oliver Cromwell was born when the sun was in Taurus, and at an hour when Aries was the Ascendant. Aries is the soldier's House, and moreover Mars was then in Aries. However, the Sun in Taurus was accompanied by two other planets, Mercury and Venus, which reinforced the earthy, stubborn and deliberate traits in Cromwell's character. Mercury lent him eloquence and a tricky nature, and Venus humanity and creative drive. So astrologers say.

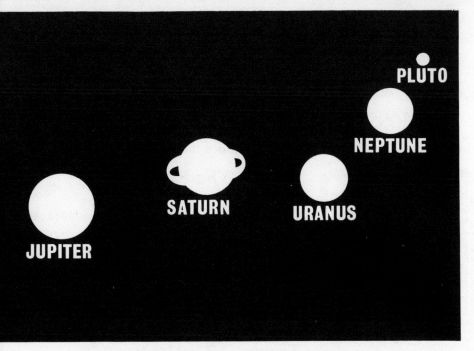

Jupiter *Majestic, virtuous, scornful, prodigal*
Saturn *Serious, thoughtful, quarrelsome, miserly*
Uranus *Kindly, creative, restless, rebellious*
Neptune *Spiritual, dreamy, luxurious, stable*
Pluto *Ambitious, tenacious, vengeful proud*

On page 232 you will find short verses describing the traditional character of the various Houses; don't pay too much attention to the dates printed with them, for these are only the dates when the Sun is in that sign. A person born between July 23rd and August 22nd may be hardly Leonine at all, if his planets and his Ascendant join to contradict the influence of the Lion.

If you want to know more about your astrological character, you must first know not only the date but also the time of your birth (if possible to within quarter of an hour) and its geographical longitude. Then you must either consult a professional astrologer or find a book containing astrological tables. These require a little mathematical knowledge to understand, but not an impossible amount. Not all books on astrology contain the tables, so check before you buy.

THE SIGNS OF THE ZODIAC

And the Characters of those born under them.

Aries—The Ram

March 21 to April 19

Quick-tempered, restless and self-willed is Aries.
Girl, if you marry him you will not marry ease.
Fickle but generous, a handsome slob,
He gives the orders and you do the job.

Taurus—The Bull

April 20 to May 19

Both earthy and stubborn is Taurus,
With a tendency also to bore us
* By his total recall*
* Of details so small*
That he's perfectly prepared to spend a whole
*   evening telling us who said what in a*
*   conversation he had sixty million years*
*   ago with a rather dull brontosaurus.*

Gemini—The Twins

May 20 to June 20

Niminy-piminy
* Flagoty Gemini*
He's a bit womany,
* She's a bit he-manny.*
Half-knowing, half-guessing,
* Half-feeling, half-thinking,*
They're in in a flash and
* They're out in a winking.*

Cancer—The Crab

June 21 to July 22

Timid and easily downcast
The gentle Crab adores the past
And cowering from the present's blast
Mourns for her shell before the last.

Leo—The Lion

July 23 to August 21

Hark to Leo's lazy roar!
See the common herd adore!
Why should Leo work to prove
That he's worthy of their love?
Leo's such a natural king
He needn't do a single thing.

Virgo—The Maiden

August 22 to September 22

Early one evening
Just as the Moon was rising
I heard the Maiden singing
  In her clear, chilly voice
"Oh, I'm so witty,
Oh, I'm so pretty,
How can it be that
  I don't get the boys?"

H*

Libra—The Scales

September 23 to October 22

In the House of Scales
Such balance prevails
That if, say, a chair
Is just here, then it's clear
That one must be there
To balance the pair.
And of much the same kind
Is the Libran in mind.
He will balance each plan
As long as he can
(Until sometimes, it's true, it
Is too late to do it.)

Scorpio—The Scorpion

October 23 to November 21

Walk ye humbly! Speak ye low!
Here comes Mr Scorpio!
For one who looks so stern and moral
He's mighty quick to pick a quarrel.

Sagittarius—The Archer

November 22 to December 21

Hurrah, hurrah for Sagittarius!
In action quick, in wit hilarious,
His virtues are so large and various
To number them would only weary us.
A snob, perhaps, but nothing serious . . .
Yes, I myself am Sagittarius!

Capricorn—The Goat

December 22 to January 20

Delightful little babies born
Under the sign of Capricorn
  May well grow up as mighty scholars.
But even if they're mighty fools
They know a thing not taught in schools—
  They know the feel and smell of dollars.

Aquarius—The Water-Bearer

January 21 to February 19

Who sits brooding all alone
  With a time-bomb in his mind?
Who runs to help the crippled crone
  And finds a pathway for the blind?
If these are truly both Aquarius
His Age may feel a mite precarious.

Pisces—The Fish

February 20 to March 20

If will *were* wish
  If dare *were* dream
These lazy fish
  Would rule the stream.

AND IS IT TRUE?

Astrology is far more widely
and deeply believed in than
either palmistry or card-reading.
In some ways this is strange,
because the planets are so far
away from us and so unalterable
in their movements, and also are
so much the same for everybody.
By contrast, the lines on my
hand belong to me alone, and so
might hold a message peculiar
to me; and at a cardreading
session my presence might
somehow influence the chance
fall of the cards.

But astrology does have some
things going for it. First it is a
good rough-and-ready way of
cataloguing different types of
character; if I think about it I can
fit most of my friends into one
house or another, especially if I
use an old text-book along with a
modern one. Modern astrologers
are rather mealy-mouthed about
characters, tending to stress all
the good points of each house,
and only to hint at the bad

*Each of the signs of the Zodiac
governs a different part of the
body*

ones, but three hundred years ago they were writing like this:

Pisces : Argueth a stammering person, one fraudulent and a Pretender to the Truth.

Virgo : One loving Learning and Arts, covetous, cruel or despightful, a well-willer to war.

Libra : One inconstant, crafty, a contemner of all Arts, conceited of his own person.

Another thing in favour of astrology is well summed up by Ptolemy, who perfected the theory about the crystal spheres that were supposed to carry the planets and stars: "A man skilled in this art may escape many of the effects of the stars, for knowing their natures he may be prepared for their effects." Each of us is, so to speak, a small boat sailing across an unknown sea, in poor visibility. All around may be rocks or currents or sea monsters, unseen in the mist. Knowledge of the stars may help us to prepare a chart, so that we can steer clear of the rocks and monsters and take advantage of the currents. But it still doesn't guarantee that we won't suffer shipwreck. It doesn't claim to tell us our destinies, and so to take our free will from us.

One curious point is that the stars that originally gave their names to the various Houses have moved. The sun does not now approach the constellation of the Bull until early May, but we still say it enters the House of the Bull on April 21. It will take 25,800 years for the Zodiac to return to its original position, and half way through that time, in about 12,000 years, each House will be exactly the opposite side of the sky to the constellation that gave it its name.

Another change has been the discovery of new planets, Uranus in 1781, Neptune in 1846 and Pluto in 1930. Astrologers have responded bravely to this challenge, giving the new planets special attributes and assigning them control over various Houses (which had to be taken away from other planets for the purpose.) Some German and American

Like this Indian seer, many palmists are also astrologers

astrologers, determined not to be caught again, have invented names and attributes for so-far-undiscovered planets, just in case.

In India, Ceylon and the Far East astrology is of real political importance. The dates for public events are chosen with the help of astrologers, and there are often bitter disputes and riots when an election-date appears to make the stars more favourable to one party than another. And there have sometimes been widespread panics in those countries, caused by a weakness, common in astrologers, for predicting the end of the world. Eastern astrologers disagree with western ones about many details of their art, but the fundamental principles, the belief in the powers and influences of the planets, are the same.

NOSTRADAMUS

In 1555 a small book was published in Lyons, France. It consisted of a short, obscure preface and three hundred four-line verses of prophecy, even more obscure. They were written by a well-known astrologer, Michel de Nostredame—Michael of Our Lady—who called himself Nostradamus. He was a very sensible kind of prophet, because he announced that though his verses were prophetic nobody would know what they foretold until after the event, so he could never be proved wrong in the way most prophets are.

A year later he was summoned to the court of King Henri II of France, and received with honour and gifts. Three years later still the king died, suddenly and nastily, and Nostradamus was able to claim that he had foretold the event in his verses. Moreover this was one of the few items in his book which he himself said applied to a specific person, the King. This is my translation:

> *The Lion young will overcome the old*
> *In field of battle by a single duel.*
> *He'll pierce his eye inside a cage of gold,*
> *Two classes one, then die a death most cruel.*

King Henri, when told that this referred to his own death, laughed and pointed out that the only words that seemed to make sense were also nonsense. He was at peace with all his neighbours, so how could he die in a field of battle?

But on July 1, 1559, Henri proclaimed a great tournament outside the walls of Paris in honour of the marriage of his daughter Elizabeth with Philip II of Spain. He himself rode in the lists, in a suit of armour fit for a great king; when the sun shone on him he dazzled the eye, a glittering man, all steel and gold. It appears that he fought well—or perhaps the knights on the other side of the barrier knew better than to unhorse their monarch. At any rate he seems to have been exhilarated with the sport, for when it was due to finish he could not bear to give the signal. The Duke of Savoy begged him to, saying that the sun was setting, and there was nothing to be gained by another running as the King's team were already victorious.

However, Henri insisted, and challenged the Captain of his Scots Guard, the Count of Montgomery, to fight one last fight. Montgomery tried to excuse himself, but then the King grew angry and swore that he would have his will. There may have been a bit of needle in this challenge, because Montgomery had rather tactlessly chosen to carry on his shield the same device as the King—a lion.

So the trumpets blew once more and the two warriors wheeled their horses out into the middle of the lists and raised their visors in salute to the Queen, Catherine de Medici. Then they took their places at opposite ends of the barrier, lowered their visors and waited. The trumpets blew for the last time, the knights spurred their horses, and the horses ramped down the lists.

Montgomery's lance took the king on the armoured throat-piece, a safe spot. The good armour held, and the lance (which was probably already half sawn through for safety) splintered. A section of the butt, cartwheeling upwards, caught the King's gilt visor and lifted it up at the exact instant that another big splinter was hurtling forwards.

This second splinter lanced through the open visor and caught the King in the eye-socket, just above the right eye. It drove in deep and pierced a major vein.

So, under a crimson sunset, that day of glamour and thrill ended in tragedy. They carried the King from the lists, and the inefficient doctors of the time managed to keep him alive for ten more days of agony. Later Montgomery was himself assassinated.

For Nostradamus, however, it was a triumph. It suddenly became obvious to all thinking men that the gold cage in the verse was the King's gilt helm, that the old lion was the King, and so Montgomery must be the young lion; so only the first three words of the last line remained obscure. They still do, though it is possible to argue that the word "classes" is Nostradamus's deliberate adaptation of a Greek word meaning "loppings". Even so, the idea of *two* loppings remained baffling until 1589, when the King's son Henri III was assassinated by a fanatical young monk. (A couple of other sons had died in the meanwhile, but if you are determined to make sense of Nostradamus you have to ignore details like that.)

Since that time a great many attempts have been made to elucidate the rest of the verses. Nostradamus published over a thousand in all, but a few have been lost. He claimed that they covered several thousand years of the future, so there is always something fresh to discover. I have on my desk two commentaries, one written nearly a hundred years ago, and the other soon after the Second World War. It is amusing to see how both commentators unconsciously assume that all the most interesting verses refer to what are to them recent events. The older author finds a lot of prophecies about rather obscure Victorian happenings, while the new one finds them about Mussolini and Hitler.

Anyway, as interpreting Nostradamus is a game that anyone can play, I've translated a set of six consecutive verses for

readers to try their hand at. Nostradamus divided his books
into sets of one hundred verses, which he called "Centuries"
though they have nothing to do with any particular century
in time. These are verses 56 to 61 of the Eighth Century,
but the events they refer to may be hundreds of years apart.
You are allowed to twist words, especially proper names,
any way you can, including making anagrams of them.
And you can assume that the words are in any language that
Nostradamus could conceivably have known. For instance,
one interpreter claims that the word "Tag" in Verse 61
refers to what the Germans called "Der Tag", that is to say
the day of vengeance and victory which they hoped would end
the first World War.

56   *The feeble troop will occupy the land.*
        Those of high place will utter frightful squeals.
      In narrow corner fret the greatest band.
        Near D. nebro he falls, the script reveals.

57   *From soldier plain he'll come to highest place.*
        To a long gown he'll come, too, from a shorter.
      Valiant at arms, in church what man more base?
        He'll vex the priests as sponge is vexed by water.

58   *Split between brothers, kingdom in debate,*
        Britannic name and weapons who's to bear.
      The English title will be told too late,
        Surprised at night and led to the French air.

59   *Lo, twice cast down and twice raised to the heights,*
        The Eastern and the Western both grow frail.
      His adversary after many fights
        Pursued at sea in utmost need shall fail.

60   *The first in Gaul, the first in Romany,*
         By sea and land, to France and Britain too,
      Marvellous deeds by that great company,
         Smashing, Norlaris Terax will undo.

61   *Never by the discovery of day*
         To sign of sceptre-bearer shall he go,
      That all his sieges be not at a stay,
         Bearing the cock the gift of Tag. Ah woe!

I've not been able to make the translations quite as obscure as the original French. Sense keeps creeping in. Most authorities agree that Verse 57 refers to Oliver Cromwell, though he was never a common soldier, and the second line doesn't fit him very well. I'd have thought almost any anti-priest soldier risen from the ranks would do—what about Leon Trotsky, for instance, who was one of the leaders of the Russian revolution, an atheist, who commanded the revolutionary armies wearing that long Russian officers' coat? 58 almost fits Edward VII's abdication as King of England. 59, 60 and 61 can be made to refer to Germany in the two World Wars. For instance, in World War Two Germany conquered France and Romania and attacked Britain. The *blitzkrieg* technique brought astonishing results ('smashing'). The Greek word for something deformed and monstrous is *teras*, so tera-X might mean a monstrous, deformed cross—the swastika. I can't make head or tail of 'Norlaris' and nor can anyone else.

Anyone who believes that the prophecies of Nostradamus do come true had better steer clear of Paris in the year 2000 A.D., when it's due to be wiped out by an atomic attack. And rockets are going to obliterate New York at some point, but he doesn't say when.

THE LINE OF LIFE

Palmistry is to my mind the hardest of the secret arts, though the easiest to believe in. Every hand is different, and even if the lines are obliterated (criminals, for instance, have tried to destroy their own fingerprints with acid) they will grow back exactly as they were. So each hand is a very personal thing, and it seems quite likely that the lines on it might convey something about its owner's character and fate.

The difficulty arises simply because all hands are different. That means that no hand conforms precisely to any set of instructions for hand-reading. The would-be palmist must learn the trade by reading hundreds of hands and interpreting tiny differences between them. Despite this difficulty, palmistry is the most settled of the secret arts; books about card-reading and astrology often disagree quite markedly about the meanings of particular signs. But palmists only differ about whether to pay more attention to the signs of character or the signs of fate.

At one time I read quite a lot of palms, and my clients would often tell me that I had foretold the same as some other palmist in their past, which was encouraging.

There's no space here for a detailed account of all the ins and outs of palmistry, and in any case it's very unlucky (tempting fate) to read your own hand. What follows is only a collection of oddments.

With right-hand people the right hand should be read, because it shows what they make of their own lives, while the left hand shows the possibilities they were born with. With left-handed people it's the other way round, but I find left-handers very much harder to read clearly.

A single line running right across the palm from side to side, instead of the usual two nearly parallel lines which start from opposite sides, used to be thought a sign of criminal degeneracy. I have one myself, and so welcome the modern theory that it may also be a sign of artistic genius.

The Line of Life is what most people are interested in. It runs from the edge of the palm between the thumb and index finger, round the ball of the thumb and down to the wrist. It is a sign of health, comfort and other physical circumstances. A line crossing it may mean some kind of illness, obstacle or problem, but a break doesn't necessarily mean death (in fact a break and a fresh start running parallel and overlapping can even be a good sign.) If you treat it as a ninety-degree arc, starting from the top, each degree is a year, roughly, but a short line doesn't mean an early death. A well-marked, clean-curving line, running widely round the ball of the thumb, is best.

Marriages and love-affairs are found on the outer edge of the palm just below the little finger; they are short, separate lines parallel to the line that marks the knuckle, and you simply number them off. The more marked they are the more serious and lasting the love. Some palmists say that the fainter lines that cross them, running up the edge of the hand, represent children—the straight ones sons and the slant ones ones daughters. If this is so, I have nine sons I know nothing about.

1. Life Line Strength of the life force, comfort, physical health—read from edge of palm down to wrist (see main text).
2. Head Line Intellectual character: e.g. a straight, clear line shows ability to concentrate. Read in contrast with heart line.
3. Heart Line Emotional character: e.g. a many-branching line shows flibbertigibbet nature.
4. Fate Line Not always present. Sometimes develops with maturity. Read up from wrist. Shows destiny, and relationship with the outside world.
5. Sun Line Not always present. Sign of fame and success.

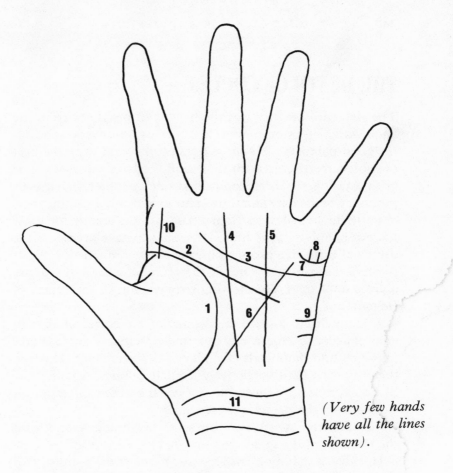

(Very few hands have all the lines shown).

6. *Health Line* A weak or broken line is bad health, a strong line or no line at all, good health.

7. *Marriage Line(s)* Marriages and love affairs. The further the line comes round to the palm, the stronger and more long-lasting the love.

8. *Children* Little lines running up from the marriage line. Vertical for boys, slant for girls.

9. *Journeys* The stronger the line the more important the journey.

10. *Money Line* Wealth and business success.

11. *Racettes* Said by some to show 25 years of life for each line.

THE DEATH OF COCLES

The sixteenth century was the heyday of prophecy from the hand, and many stories are told of the astounding accuracy of the great palmists. Of course feats of this kind were the best possible advertisement for their skill. Perhaps this is why the great astrologer Cardan committed suicide rather than see his prophecy of the date and time of his own death not come true.

Barthelmy Cocles, an Italian palmist, was among the most famous palmists of his time. He is said to have predicted the deaths of forty-five people, only two of whom failed to die at the time he had said. One of the remaining forty-three was a great nobleman, Hermes Bentivoglio, son of the tyrant of Bologna.

It is unwise to foresee the destiny of the powerful. A man who expects to rule a city for many years, is not grateful for being told that his days of glory will never come. Hearing the prophecy, Bentivoglio frowned like thunder. An officer of his court, called the constable, noticed the frown and followed Cocles from the prince's presence.

"You there," he called, "Sir seer! If you are so free with the fortunes of the great, you may tell my fortune also."

His idea at that moment was only to mock the palmist, and show his scorn by paying him at the end with the smallest copper coin in his purse. Cocles (a contemporary picture shows him as a mild-looking little man, large-eyed, clean-shaven and wizened) turned back towards the bullying voice, politely took the outstretched hand and peered at it, muttering under his breath. But in a very few seconds he dropped the hand and turned away again.

"Well?" barked the constable.

Cocles paused in his stride and half turned.

"In eight days," he said, "you will commit a most detestable murder."

Then he walked away, before the amazed constable could

begin to fumble in his purse. That happened on the 16th of September, 1504.

On the 24th Cocles left his study, as usual, to sup at a nearby tavern. His manservant was astonished to see the mild little scholar leave the house wearing a soldier's steel helmet and carrying a sword.

Who knows? Perhaps even till then the constable had intended to do no more that frighten the prophet by giving him a thorough beating. Perhaps it was the sight of the sword and helmet that turned the thrashing into brutal murder. Or perhaps the original prophecy had put the idea into the man's dull mind. At any rate when his master did not come home Cocles' servant went out to look for him, and found his body in an alleyway, with the head savagely beaten in. The old man had never drawn his sword and the useless helmet lay beside him in the gutter.

The Zoo in Your Dreams

Dream of a crocodile, wake to danger.
Dream of a lobster and wake to wealth.
Dream of a dog and you'll meet a stranger.
Dream of a frog and you'll know good health.

Dream of a squirrel—your hopes mount higher.
Dream of an eagle and grow to fame.
Dream of a wolf and you'll meet a liar.
(Dream mice or monkeys for much the same.)

Dream of a bear and it's odds agin' you.
Dream of a bull and a rival's there.
Dream of a swan and pleasure will win you.
Dream of a shark and you'll know despair.

Dream of beetles and worries arise.
Dream of a fish for a nice surprise.

A blind man stands in the sunlight,
leaning on his stick, thinking. The
dust of the road is soft beneath his
naked soles; the sun strikes warm
along his flank; the dry hillside above
him also warms its flank and begins to smell of
morning, the odours of the Greek hills that he barely noticed
when he had his sight.

His eyes have stopped hurting; there is only the ache in his
mind. He still has his inward vision, too. He remembers the
tired priestess swaying on the three-legged frame work that
held her above the crack where the vapours rose in the cave.
He can see her body suddenly stiffen as she feels his presence

until she balances there rigid as a temple pillar. He can see her froth-ringed lips open wide, impossibly wide, so that she can speak with the voice of the God.

But now he stands relaxed in the sunlight, thinking back down his days, from the chance that saw him born into the palace at Thebes, through the luck (first bad, then good) that carried him to the palace at Corinth, to the destiny that brought him to face the stare of the Sphinx). He sighs and turns his other flank to the sun. Then he smiles, re-membering that Apollo, the sun-god who warms him, is the same God who spoke through the lips of the priestess and foresaw it all. What can Apollo see now for a blind man who has fulfilled his mysterious purpose?

Nothing. There is nothing for him to do but wait in the sun for a sign, quiet and patient, like a man watching a tuft of thistledown eddy along a hill ridge.

Out of the distance, but clear and clearer (his hearing has become more keen with every day of blindness) footsteps approach along the road, bare feet treading softly in the dust.

"Good morning," he says.

"Good morning," says a woman's voice. "Do you need help, old man?"

(Old? A month ago he was a king, young and strong.)

"Only to know where this road leads," he says.

"Which road do you want?" she answers. "You are at a cross-roads, old man."

For a moment he stands frozen, as though struck with the shaft of the God. Then he smiles. The Gods have done all they can to him, but still he is alive, standing in the sunlight, at a crossroads. A sign has been sent. Here, once more, the linked network of destinies begins.

The woman tells him what villages the roads lead to. He chooses without thought, thanks her and begins to feel his way forward. His staff prods blindly for footing, but his limbs seem slowly to lose the tired shuffle of defeat, and he moves on with increasing confidence to encounter fresh chances, new luck, another destiny.

THE BARROW-MOUND

Reason is king, but still
  Beyond wait mysteries.
Under the man-piled hill
  A burial lies,
Bones that obeyed one will,
  Skull that had eyes.

Eyes frowning at the stars,
  Curious to mark
The erratic path of Mars—
  Then just a nameless spark—
Will to begin to parse
  The grammar of the dark.

Since no historian
  Knows at what date
(Dim as the future) man
  First mapped the great,
Intricate, star-formed plan
  We call our fate.

What harm is it to guess
  This barrow-king
Discerned in randomness
  A patterning
And earned his burial place
  By that one thing?

And what if he was wrong?
  He was well called wise
In his own time, who on
  The chance-strewn skies
Imposed in myth and song
  Huge destinies

King Reason lies below
  Just such a mound,
Man-piled. How, Such and So—
  All we have found,
All that we think we know—
Bury his dry bones, though
Star-worlds of mystery glow
  Beyond, beyond.